A Garden Full of Flowers

Violet Stevenson

and Flowers without a Garden

Hamlyn

LONDON · NEW YORK · SYDNEY · TORONTO

Contents

Acknowledgements
We should like to thank the following
for the photographs in this book:
Colour: Pat Brindley, John Cowley,
Leslie Johns and Harry Smith.
Black and white: Pat Brindley, Ernest
Crowson, A. J. Huxley, Elsa M. Megson
and Harry Smith

First published in paperback form in 1968
Revised and published in hardback form
in 1975 by
The Hamlyn Publishing Group Limited
London · New York · Sydney · Toronto
© Copyright Violet Stevenson 1968, 1975

Filmset in 11 on 13 pt. Monophoto
Photina by
Filmtype Services Ltd, Scarborough,
England
Printed and bound in
The Canary Islands by
Litografia A. Romero, S.A. Santa Cruz de
Tenerife, Canary Islands (Spain) D. L. TF. 687-1975

ISBN 0 600 30243 1

Introduction

In writing this book I have been guided by the knowledge that most gardeners grow plants for their flowers and usually that the more blooms a plant will produce the more highly it is regarded. This is confirmed by the thousands of letters I have received over the years from readers of my books and articles. For myself, there are many plants which I grow in my own garden for the sake of their leaves, because I need the form, texture and subdued colours they bring to flower arrangements. These are chosen simply because, like many of our favourite house plants, they have beautiful and long-lasting foliage. Often, though, it happens that unlike most of the kinds grown indoors, a garden foliage plant will also produce lovely blooms, thus giving a double service. Hostas, bergenias, annual poppies and alchemilla are examples. Naturally, these are one's first choice.

My own garden is filled with flowering plants of many kinds and there is not a day of the year without some flower in bloom, even though, like the winter-flowering heathers, it may be under the snow, ready to colour the border after the thaw.

Flowers are so easy to come by. Even those who have never gardened before and who perhaps have taken on a newly built house and an uncultivated plot of land can have a garden full of flowers within a few months by planting shrubs, particularly roses (how quickly a new estate becomes floral!), by broadcasting annual seed even over uncultivated land in some cases, and by planting bulbs.

With the widespread establishment of garden centres it is now possible to buy plants which are in bloom and to plant them right away. These have been grown for a long period in containers and they receive no check when they are properly planted and watered.

There are other marketed items which minimise losses and help cut out weary labour. There are such products as ready-mixed seed, cutting and potting composts, good basic fertilizers, handy sprays of insecticides and others.

Our seedsmen market a wonderful variety of seeds, all of which are extremely cheap, even in today's inflationary world. Bulb merchants offer both the everyday familiar species and new varieties and novelties. All these things make gardening easier and they also make it a little more exciting. I try always to grow at least one new flower each year and I try also to go back in time to find an old favourite which seems shyly to have taken a back seat.

Of course a great deal depends upon the size of a garden. But you can have flowers even without one. This book should help those who have instead to use the walls of their house, the paving around it or the window-sills.

For those who have really large plots I would urge that apart from making a garden where the choicest of cultivated plants grow happily, they cast their thoughts beyond the boundaries of their plot and consider their countryside at large. It takes but little room or labour to allow a few native plants to grow and increase. If these should also be host plants for certain species of moths and butterflies, or the basic food of birds, so much the better, for one will thus be strengthening the links in the chain of life which at times seems perilously to be weakening at certain points.

Since my husband and I made our garden, we have watched the number of wild fauna grow around us. We read in newspapers of disappearing butterflies and step out into a garden where in their seasons there are always some to be seen. We know that this is because we grow or allow to grow certain native plants which are vital to them. It so happens that these plants are mainly attractive or useful. The exceptions are nettles, although even these can be eaten should you so wish! So far as conservation is concerned I think that gardeners can play an important role and it is wonderful to think that they can do this by growing flowers.

So, this is a book all about flowers. Flowers for everyone, everywhere. Because I know from experience that many of the common or folk names of plants, much as I love them, can cause confusion, I have used the correct botanical names throughout. Where possible I have also given the trivial or familiar name, but one should realize that this can vary from place to place.

I hope this book lives up to its promise — a profusion of flowers, bringing the magic of their colour and perfume to your garden, your home and your life.

Violet Stevenson

Flowers from Bulbs and Corms

Spring and Early Summer

Few experiences are as rewarding as growing flowers from bulbs and corms. These are nature's prepacks, each one a compact little bundle of glories to come, for in each specimen is a potential flower, sometimes many flowers.

Growing bulbs entails easy gardening with the maximum effect. Some are easier to grow than others; most come up year after year increasing themselves in various ways meanwhile.

Although many bulb plants like a sunny spot they will also grow in shade or partial shade. They are very obliging and will grow in most soils, but they prefer a porous, well-drained site to a heavy or waterlogged soil. Humus in the soil will not only improve it but will also aid porosity. While you should never use fresh manure on bulb soil, well-rotted dung, garden compost, peat and leafmould are all ideal and should be used liberally on heavy soils. (Throughout this book, when I mention manures and home-made garden composts I mean well-rotted samples only. Fresh dung can be injurious.)

With a little planning you can have flowers from bulbs the whole year through. In my own garden spring begins early in January with snowdrops and crocus species followed by aconites, other types of crocus, the first narcissi, early tulips, scillas, the tiny fairy-like irises, chionodoxas and many others, with the various types of narcissi and tulips in flower all the time, right through until the summer-flowering bulbs begin to show above ground.

In June come the Dutch and the English iris; in July there are lilies followed by gladioli, *Hyacinthus candicans*, chincherinchees, and so on in a charming sequence to the end of the year when the snowdrops begin to appear again.

My advice to the new gardener is to get a catalogue from one of the leading bulb merchants. These publications are not only helpful but interesting. Often beautifully produced, they create impulse buying like the supermarkets! At least they always seem to tempt me, but I have never regretted money spent on bulbs. And here I must stress that it always pays to buy good-quality bulbs. Bargain offers must be approached with caution. No bulb will flower until it reaches a certain age, during which time it must be grown under perfect conditions. Those you buy from a reputable merchant are certain to flower. Indeed, on the bulb field, the year before the bulb is sold, it is allowed to show its bloom as a proof of its variety. The bloom is then removed so that all the strength and resources of the plant are diverted back to the bulb.

Very cheap lines are likely to be those which are too young or small to bloom. On the other hand, bulbs are often sold at reduced prices at the end of a season. Although they will be planted later than is ideal, these can be good buys but do not expect them to flower at exactly the proper season.

Botanically speaking there are three types of these food-storing plants: bulbs, corms and tubers. But generally you are likely to find them all grouped under the omnibus heading of 'bulbs' and, in the main, they all need much the same treatment.

Not only do bulbs provide us with many types of flowers, but they lend themselves to many uses in the garden. Remember that the most sophisticated are the most adaptable and that those usually seen growing in a natural manner or 'wild' are likely to be more set in their ways. Some kinds can play many roles and are described in later chapters. In the tiny town garden bulbs can be used to bring scent and colour to troughs, beds, tubs, terrace vases, even window-boxes.

In the garden there are enough for both formal and informal schemes. For instance, a formal bed looks best filled with tulips, while scillas of various colours will look best under small trees and shrubs. The rock garden gives one another place in which to show off the little ones to advantage. So does an alpine house (see my notes in Chapter 16, 'Flowers from Bulbs to Grow Indoors'). A bed near the water garden can be a marvellous spot for others. One of the prettiest settings I remember was of a group of crown imperials growing so near a pool (but not in moist soil) that they were reflected in its water.

Large-flowered bulbs such as tulips, narcissi, iris and gladioli are improved if they are not allowed to make seed. Remove the faded flower head or spike as early as possible. Small-flowered kinds, especially those 'naturalized', should be allowed to seed.

The important thing at any time when buying your bulbs is to get them out of their bags or boxes as quickly as possible. Even if you have no time at the moment to plant them, you should open the bag to let the air in, or, better still, remove the bulbs and lay them out in trays or put them in string bags.

As a general rule plant all bulbs so that the tip is one and a half times their full depth below soil level. For instance, if a bulb is 2 in. from tip to base its tip should be planted 3 in. below the soil. They can be set quite close to one another, but allow for growth. Except in very light sandy soils, where the particles

The starry-eyed little blue and white chionodoxas add charm to the display of spring-flowering bulbs

run freely when dry, all bulbs should be planted with a trowel and not a dibber. I like the specially designed bulb-planting trowel which is narrower than the usual design. You can get some bulb planters marked in inches.

On all heavy, sticky soils and especially where slugs are present, I strongly advise that all bulbs should be sat on a little cushion of coarse, clean, sand when they are planted.

Possibly one great advantage that the spring-flowering kinds have over other plants for the tidy gardener is that they can be lifted when they fade and begin to look shabby, to make room for herbaceous, annual and summer bedding plants.

You must make up your mind on whether or not the bulbs you buy are to be expendable, for this will depend upon your budget as well as the type of garden you have. Some people prefer to throw them out at the end of each season and begin afresh each year. As a rule this happens in formal gardens where the beds are cleared as the flowers fade and are then replanted.

On the other hand, if you want to you can grow

7

most of the bulbs year after year. Naturalized bulbs, those planted in areas which are left undisturbed or mainly so, seldom need any attention. Little bulb flowers make delightful ground cover — you have only to think of bluebell woods to realise how effective these can be.

I hesitate to recommend growing narcissi in grass, although they look so pretty, because in my own experience they tend to deteriorate through starvation as the bulbs become crowded. You can get around this by lifting them every few years, separating the crowded clumps, enriching the soil with a little bonemeal and replanting thinly. Another disadvantage is that the grass should not be mown until the leaves of the bulbs die down naturally.

Although my husband and I have given up growing daffodils in grass we do like an informal effect. This we have achieved by planting all kinds of narcissi in zones quite near the back edges of the borders which meander down the length of the garden. In spring we see charming drifts of colour which, because the flowers meander with the lines of the border, seem to mingle with the shrubs and grass. The advantage of this method is that as the bulbs become crowded it is quite a simple matter, even when the border is full of plants, to lift them, return a few to the original area near the edge and then plant the surplus elsewhere.

Even bulbs which are usually left undisturbed give bigger and better flowers if they are divided occasionally. I always divide some muscari (grape hyacinths) and *Scilla campanulata*, correctly known now as *Endymion hispanicus*. I am gradually extending the drift of snowdrops along our south-facing hedgerow by lifting a few clumps immediately after flowering, and replanting small handfuls further along. But where I want the flowers to carpet the soil I leave them alone. I never touch lilies either.

From this you will see that it does most bulbs little harm to be lifted. With some it is important not to lift them too soon and I will deal with these as I come to them. The most important point to emphasize now is that you should handle the foliage as carefully as you can. If care is not taken the bulbs will ultimately die. This is why bluebell woods go on being filled with flowers provided only the blooms are gathered, but once the leaves are trampled on and destroyed the plant dies and in time the woods lose their lovely floral carpet.

Foliage is essential to the development of the bulb and the following year's flowers, so when you cut flowers for the house you should cut short stems, leaving plenty of foliage on the stems. (It is therefore sensible to make a cutting border where the bulbs are expendable.)

If bulbs are lifted from a bed to make way for other plants, they must be allowed to continue to grow somewhere so that their leaves will die down naturally. They should *not* be lifted green and then put somewhere to dry. In most gardens a little area out of sight can be selected for the purpose of finishing off the bulbs. Here they can be planted much closer than they were formerly.

I make trenches across the plot. The best way is to begin at the back and dig a spit-deep trench. Into this I throw a little mixed peat and sand to discourage slugs. The lifted bulbs are laid against the far side of the trench and covered with the soil removed in making the next trench. Remember to keep the varieties separate and marked in some way. A piece of polythene or wire netting will make an easy division.

You will be able to tell when the leaves have done their job, for you can pull them easily from the top of the bulb without tugging. The bulbs are now 'ripe'. Lift them and spread them out to dry in the air. Make sure that they are not allowed to lie in the hot sun for a long period or you will kill the outer scales.

Clean and sort them when they are dry to the touch. Try to keep them as complete as possible but remove any loose skin or 'tunics'. Separate parents from off-sets when these exist but only pull apart any portions which come away easily. Mature narcissi for example are often 'double-nosed'.

Select the largest for replanting in the beds and put aside the others to plant in cutting borders or in a row where they can be left undisturbed until they are large enough to bloom well. Many immature bulbs produce tiny flowers. 'Spawn', the tiny bulbils formed round some mother bulbs, should be sown in a row like peas. Until planting time, store in trays or string bags hung up in a dry, airy shed.

Although I have given you the ideal methods for lifting and dividing bulbs I must confess that I do not always follow the rules myself, usually simply because if the job isn't done when I see that it needs doing there may not be time at the proper season. For years I have successfully moved and sometimes divided and re-planted bulbs, including narcissi and tulips, when they have just appeared above the soil, when they have been in bud, in flower and immediately after flowering.

Although the easiest way to grow bulbs is to leave them in the soil for several years without giving them any attention, there are a few disadvantages. In country gardens, tulip and crocus bulbs are eaten by field mice, and in heavy soils slugs can be a great nuisance — one good reason why one should try to change the character of the soil.

NARCISSI. The most familiar of all spring-flowering bulbs are those of the great narcissi family. As a rule, we call the kinds with long trumpets daffodils, and those with short cups narcissi, but since all are one and the same thing, narcissi being the botanical name, there is no set rule. Narcissi bulbs should be planted as early as possible. They are best lifted and divided roughly every three years. I am happy that the deep, rather stiff though humusy soil of my cottage garden is the soil narcissi prefer. The trumpet daffodils seem the most adaptable. The *poeticus* varieties prefer a really humusy soil.

The glorious flowers we now grow are the results of generations of hybridization. (This flower incidentally, often will hybridize itself in a wild state if two species grow near each other.) In fact, so varied have they become that The Royal Horti-

In a small garden narcissi look happiest planted among shrubs or beside a path where they can be left undisturbed and do not have to be moved to make room for bedding plants

cultural Society has classified narcissi according to certain characteristics. There are now eleven well-defined groups or classes, ranging from Class 1 for trumpet varieties, through large and small cups, plain and coloured, doubles, *triandrus*, species and others. These classifications need not concern the ordinary gardener who does not intend to exhibit his or her flowers, but I explain them here because the flowers are often classified in this manner in bulb catalogues.

If you like variety you can find it among the narcissi. There are yellow daffodils with trumpet or corona and matching perianth (the term for the 'petal' part). Bicolours have trumpets of one colour, perianths of another, and there are those with white trumpets. I have drifts of Beersheba, one of my favourites, planted among the shrubs in my mainly silver border. Here I have a deciduous variegated dogwood, with bright ruby-coloured bark in winter, and the colour contrast of the young

Bottom: Narcissi are delightful when naturalized in grass. To avoid starvation, the bulbs should be lifted and replanted every few years

Opposite left: *Colchicum speciosum*, the meadow saffron, is not unlike a crocus but has larger blooms. It flowers at the end of summer

Opposite right: The charming winter aconite, or eranthis, makes a lovely spring carpet under trees. This is *Eranthis tubergenii*, a hybrid

Opposite bottom: The magnificent summer-flowering *Lilium auratum* prefers an acid soil. Like many bulbs, lilies seem to thrive best when planted among shrubs where the soil around their roots can be left undisturbed

bright stems and the pale daffodils is very lovely, especially as both rise up from a ground cover of blue forget-me-nots.

I am proud of the fact that I once worked in the nursery where Fortune, the first narcissus with a bright orange corona, was 'born'. This, incidentally, is a fine variety for a cool, damp part of the garden. With these and with all the yellow varieties I grow the purple biennial honesty, which, after flowering and gloriously complementing the bulb flowers, will hide their fading foliage with its own purpling leaves and handsome seed pods.

Other narcissi have a white perianth and coloured corona. Some of these are very beautiful indeed, John Evelyn for example, which is a very good naturalizing variety, and has a snow-white perianth round a flat, open, apricot-orange crown which is prettily frilled. There are pink varieties, some of them still a little expensive since they are still so new, which are delightful for the flower arranger. The most famous (and a cheap one!), Mrs R. O. Backhouse, has an ivory-white perianth around an elegant corona of pale rosy apricot.

There are double narcissi for those who like them and in this section is one of the sweetest scented of them all, *Narcissus albus plenus odoratus* or the double white *poeticus* which flowers late, in May.

The jonquils and their hybrids include some of the most graceful of narcissi. The *tazetta* hybrids are ideal for growing indoors. Many of them have flowers which grow in bunches and are known as polyanthus-flowered.

Narcissus cyclamineus, so named because of the way the perianth turns back like a cyclamen, has hybrids which are the earliest flowering of the narcissi such as February Gold, Peeping Tom, and March Sunshine, all of which will last several weeks in bloom.

Some of the species are doll sized and may be grown on rock gardens or in pots in alpine houses or they may be naturalized in tiny alpine meadows. You can see these at The Royal Horticultural Society gardens at Wisley in Surrey, covering the ground in the low grass with other tiny spring flowers.

TULIPS. These are as varied as the narcissi, and new varieties and hybrids are constantly appearing.

We have the Early-flowering kinds, single and double. These are really very early and many of them are good for forcing. Mendel or Mid-season tulips are single, tall and of medium build, the result of a cross between Duc van Tol and Darwin tulips.

These also are particularly valuable for forcing. Triumph tulips, and Mid-season, are also single and tall but stouter than the Mendels. May-flowering and Cottage tulips, which include the Lily-flowered, those with the tips of their petals turned back, are less formal and very pretty grown among other plants.

Dutch and English Breeders are beautifully coloured with oval flowers and can be distinguished from other kinds by their brown, red, purple or even bronze petals. Darwin tulips are perhaps the most familiar. These are almost square. They have strong, tall stems, and are beloved by parks' gardeners who often plant them so that they rise high and handsome above a floral carpet of some herbaceous plant closely planted below them.

Some years ago, when I was in Holland, a friend took me to see a Dutch hybridist who was raising some very exciting flowers. In a little bed, hidden away behind his house, was a patch of the biggest and brightest tulips I had ever seen. They were the first Fosteriana hybrids, now familiar to most gardeners but quite revolutionary then. Now many of this type are grown in our gardens; they flower very early and are gloriously coloured.

Darwin hybrids are the results of crossing Darwin tulips with these *T. fosteriana* (the species itself comes in a later section of this chapter). They flower just after the early singles and before the true Darwins and are simply gorgeous.

Then come Broken Dutch Breeders, Broken English Breeders and the Rembrandt or Bizarre tulips. The term 'broken' refers (of all things!) to the colour, the main colour being broken by slashings of other colours. These tulips are very unusual and I love them for flower arrangement but they are more expensive than the other types.

The flamboyant Parrot or Dragon varieties have feathered petals and broken colours and flower in May. The Late Double tulips, almost peony sized, make a wonderful show in late April. I have some planted among peonies in a bed, for the flowers are similar and the peony foliage hides the fading tulips' leaves.

The last section includes species and first crosses between species, many of them ideal for rock gardens. Here I should say that we can expect to see many more interesting and beautiful flowers in the coming years.

The Fosteriana hybrids I mentioned earlier fall into this division and these are both early and showy; indeed they come so early that the great

Tulipa kaufmanniana is sometimes known as the water-lily
tulip because of the way the petals open wide to the sun.
It is equally at home in the rock garden or the border

blooms are often badly damaged by wind, so give
them shelter.

The Greigii hybrids, sometimes called Peacock
tulips, are prettily tinted in primrose, cream,
scarlet and orange, usually with a vivid area down
the centre of the petal, though they may be striped
in varying degrees according to the variety. The
dark green foliage is distinctive, being handsomely
and sometimes very boldly mottled with violet-
brown markings. This means that the plant is
decorative even when it is not in bloom. The Kaufmanniana hybrids are the water-lily tulips, so called
because of the lovely way they open wide to the sun.
These are beautiful both for beds and rock gardens
where they will colour a small patch of ground with
flowers that open wide and touch petal to petal tip.
They are doubly valuable because they flower so
early, in March. Many of these tulips also have
mottled or striped leaves.

Some bulb merchants group all species tulips as
'botanical' tulips — I presume because they have
not yet given rise to varieties with homely names.
If you are interested in flowers for the rock garden
do study this section carefully for you can find
some real treasures.

Tulips will grow in most soils but they are
generally a little more tricky than narcissi simply
because they succumb more easily to disease if
proper care is not taken. Soil becomes 'sick' when
tulips are grown in it year after year. If you hope
to grow them continually in the same bed the best
way is to cover the soil surface with a deep mulch
of peat or coconut fibre after planting. When the
bulbs are lifted this mulch and any fallen leaves or
petals should be raked off and burned.

If, in the past, you have found that tulips do
become diseased in your garden, treat the bulbs
before planting with Botrilex, a non-poisonous
fungicide. Follow the directions on the packet —
1 lb. will dust 500 bulbs.

As with so many other flowers it is not possible
to lay down hard and fast rules. Some tulips will
come up year after year. We have some in our
rose bed where the bulbs are buried so deep that we
are afraid that we will kill the roses if we search
for them, so they stay and bloom happily.

Tulips like a well-drained sandy soil. The bulbs
are best not planted early or their young growth
may become damaged by frosts and subsequently
by fire, the name given to a particularly virulent
fungus disease which affects them.

CROCUS. The gay crocuses are surely the first
signs that spring is really on the way! Those that
carpet our park lawns so prettily are usually the
large-flowered Dutch hybrids which begin blooming in March and carry on into early April. There
are many lovely varieties of white, yellow and
purple in many tints and tones and some are
striped.

These crocuses will grow well in almost any soil
or situation and, since each corm produces a
succession of flowers, you get real value for money,
but do watch out for mice! All crocuses may be left
undisturbed for years or they may be lifted. To
increase your stock, lift the corms when they have
died down naturally and remove the young ones,
formed either on top or on the side of the parent
corm. When you plant these, allow room for them
to expand.

There are crocus species which flower much
earlier than the Dutch hybrids, some of these
coming under the classification of autumn-flowering species. If you live in a cold part of the country
grow these in pans or in a cold frame so that they
can be protected in really cold weather.

The endearing little *Crocus chrysanthus* will
bloom as early as January. The flowers seem to rush
into bloom — one day there are none and the next,

Left: An herbaceous border at the height of summer, with lychnis, asters, lysimachias, geraniums, heleniums and delphiniums. Many of these perennial plants can be grown from seed, though some may be slow to germinate

Top: Most annuals and bedding plants can be easily raised from seed. In this colourful border are verbenas, tagetes, nicotianas, antirrhinums and pelargoniums

Right: *Chaenomeles speciosa* Knap Hill Scarlet, one of the best of the japonicas or Japanese quinces. The lovely waxy flowers are followed in late summer by greenish fruits

or so it seems, the ground is carpeted with the long blooms which open wide to the sun as they become older. I always plant a patch near the house where I can see them from the windows. Annuals planted over them will keep their place in summer.

Even where it grows wild in its native Greece and Asia Minor, *C. chrysanthus* is very variable in colouring. This may be one reason why so very many beautiful seedlings have been raised – white, primrose, yellow, gold and bronze, as well as blues and mauves in many pastel tints. Smaller than the Dutch hybrids, they make up for this in quantity and most of them produce clusters of lovely little flowers.

Other species which flower early include *C. sieberi*, lavender with deep interior, end of February; *C. susianus*, the Cloth of Gold crocus, mid-February; and *C. tomasinianus*, a sapphire-lavender species with varieties of other hues, March flowering.

If you want to plant the species on the rock garden make sure that you prepare the site well. Mix in plenty of small stones (washed shingle will do), so that it is well drained. If you plant the corms a little deeper than is recommended you can plant dwarf-growing alpines above them. The crocuses will grow up through them and colour the cover plant prettily. Be prepared for them to pop up unexpectedly in other places because the corms travel underground as they are propagated, being gradually pushed away from the parent corm.

IRISES. Gardeners familiar only with the splendid bearded irises or flags are often surprised to find what a great number there are which can be raised from bulbs and not from rhizomes (the thick roots produced by the other types). In fact, there are so many irises of all kinds, bulbous and otherwise, that it is possible to have them in flower for every month of the year.

Furthermore, they are so adaptable. The dwarf, bulbous, spring-flowering irises may be planted in the sun, or the rock garden, on a raised bed or among shrubs in partial shade. The advantages of the method are that their colour is richer and that the flowering period is extended. They can also be grown in pots.

Violet-scented *Iris reticulata* flowers as early as January, February or March according to the severity of the season or your locality. There are many varieties of *reticulata* and although the deep purple ones are lovely they do not always show up well in a garden (though they are delightful in pans). Cantab, a paler blue, is better.

Lavender-blue, violet-scented *I. bakeriana* blooms in January or February; *I. histrioides* is an attractive 12-in.-high royal-blue and gold species and flowers in January. Flowering at the same time, *I. danfordiae* gleams in the winter gloom, even though it is only 3 in. high; this species is a little more robust in appearance than *reticulata* but still very dainty and ideal for rock gardens.

Dutch iris are hybrids which have a little of the Spanish iris strain in them. They are very handsome. They bloom from May onwards although some, notably the varieties Wedgwood and Imperator, are good for forcing. The bulbs should be planted in September and October, in gritty soil – they must have well-drained soil to do well.

HYACINTHS. So popular for indoor decoration, hyacinths are sometimes overlooked for the garden, yet no spring flower is more opulent.

A member of the lily tribe, the hyacinth is closely related to the scillas and the chionodoxas. Another member of the lily family, the muscari, shares the hyacinth's name. There are grape, tassel, feather and musk hyacinths, but botanically these are not the same as the true *Hyacinthus orientalis*, from which the showy lovely flowers have been raised.

Hyacinths are a garden luxury. They really should be planted anew each year, because as the years go by fewer and fewer flowers appear on their stems.

Hyacinths like a rich soil which is also light and well drained. In cold districts it is wise to cover them with litter or leaves during winter.

MUSCARI. This family was given its name because of the musky scent of some species. Grape hyacinths were called this because the tiny flowers are clustered in a grape-like bunch. I find them agreeable and adaptable. They don't resent being moved in full flower, something I have done sometimes when planning a new part of the garden.

They will grow in almost any soil or situation, but they do best and certainly increase more rapidly in rich, well-drained soil. Lift the bulbs in July or August, if you wish to find offsets, but I always lift and divide immediately after flowering.

The bulb merchants offer *Muscari armeniacum* in many blues. *M. botryoides album*, or Pearls of Spain, is white and fragrant.

M. comosum plumosum (syn. *monstrosum*) is the feather hyacinth with plume-like flowers. Violet-blue *M. latifolium* is one of the largest of the species. *M. paradoxum* and the sweetly scented *racemosum* and *tubergenianum* are unusual species you might

like to try. Both are suitable for the rock garden.

SCILLAS. To most people scillas are the tiny flowers of vivid blue which appear in March or early April. Blue snowdrops, as a little child once described them to me, they do resemble the little bowed heads of the white flowers, but the latter belongs to the amaryllis family, while the scillas are the lily's cousins. *Scilla siberica* and *S. bifolia* are the early-flowering species.

These will grow well in any ordinary soil. You can plant *S. bifolia* with winter aconites so that both are in bloom in February, making a charming picture. There is a *rosea* form of *bifolia*, really a purple pink. *S. pratensis*, May flowering, is good for a rock garden.

Scilla campanulata, similar in appearance to the wild bluebells of our woods, is also sometimes called *S. hispanica*, hence the more homely name of Spanish bluebells. If you want the wild bluebell, really endymion, you are likely to find it catalogued under *S. nutans*.

SNOWDROPS. When we first bought our tiny cottage we found by early spring that we had also bought, unawares, hundreds of snowdrops, *Galanthus nivalis*, which still bloom and seed every year.

Muscari botryoides album, the white form of the grape hyacinth. Muscari will grow in most soils and situations

To the original colony I have added other kinds, including the old-fashioned double snowdrop which I rescued in full bloom from the site of an old cottage across the fields, where tree felling was in progress.

A few growers specialize in these flowers. General bulb merchants list only few. *G. elwesii* flowers in January and February, is one of the largest flowered species and is also one which (unlike the others) prefers a warm and sunny site to a shady or even semi-shady position. S. Arnott is the largest variety — the stems are 10 in. high and the flowers are very sweetly scented. *G. n. viridapicis* has green-tipped petals.

Plant the bulbs early and remember that they are happier among shrubs or in grass. Allow them to grow undisturbed, but if you do want to move or divide them, lift them immediately after flowering and pull the clumps apart. Make sure that you replant to the original depth, shown by the pale portion of the stem.

LEUCOJUMS. Similar to the snowdrop in appearance, except that the inner cup is much larger and that there are two or more flowers to a longer stem, are the snowflakes or leucojum. *Leucojum vernum*, the spring snowflake, blooms in February and March. *L. aestivum* and Gravetye Variety flower in April and May.

These will grow in any ordinary, well-drained soil. They prefer shady rather than sunny positions, and the less they are disturbed the better.

ALLIUMS. The faithful onion has many grand cousins which are well worth growing. They all like light, well-drained soil. From March to May the white heads of 12-in.-high *Allium neapolitanum grandiflorum* (also a good pot plant) will shine wherever it is given a well-drained site in the open. In May, growing up from very broad, flat, blue-green leaves, *A. karataviense* bears dense round umbels of white flowers on 6-in. stems. *A. ostrowskianum* is only 6 in. high but has immense umbels.

In June the others bloom. *A. moly*, with bright yellow umbels, will continue to appear year after year. *A. albopilosum* is a giant flower consisting of a perfectly round head composed of stars of silver-lilac on 2-ft.-high stems. *A. caeruleum* (sometimes called *azureum*) has sky-blue flowers. *A. roseum* is good for cutting. It has slender 12-in stems and soft rose flowers.

Most of these propagate themselves by offsets which can be separated from the parent bulbs after the plants have died down. Some species produce tiny bulbils in the flower portion, and you can collect these and sow separately.

ORNITHOGALUMS. The name Star of Bethlehem suits these pretty flowers. They are hardy and free flowering, and are good plants for naturalizing in among shrubs, under trees in grass, as well as in borders. The soil must be well drained. The three you are most likely to find listed are: *Ornithogalum arabicum*, May and June; *O. nutans*, April and May; *O. umbellatum*, the Star of Bethlehem, May; and *O. thyrsoides*, the chincherinchee.

FRITILLARIAS. It never ceases to fascinate me that a plant as exotic in appearance as the crown imperial, *Fritillaria imperialis*, should also look so much at home in our cottage gardens. But alas,

A good plant for naturalizing in grass or among shrubs is *Ornithogalum thyrsoides*, the chincherinchee

there is none in mine! Those I planted in the early days just could not take the heavy soil as it was then. Now, after many years of cultivation the soil is much improved, lilies are growing successfully and so I feel that we can move on soon to crown imperials.

The trouble with heavy soils is that they are also wet. The moisture tends to collect in the centres of the fleshy bulbs and causes them to decay. It is said that a way of preventing wet rot is to plant the bulb on its side. Although these flowers will grow in ordinary soils, those which are neither acid nor limy, a rich soil is essential.

A shady position is best. To maintain soil richness, topdress with manure or garden compost each year. The bulbs should be left as undisturbed as possible, and should not be transplanted more often than once every four years, but if you have some growing well try to avoid even this.

There are several varieties ranging from yellow to red orange.

Fritillaria citrina, persica and the snake's-head fritillary, *meleagris,* and many others which are rarer, are much smaller species but still very distinctive. These three also flower in May but usually begin blooming in April. They look best in groups or drifts in borders in partial shade or, alternatively, on the rock garden. *F. meleagris* is delightful when naturalized. There are now several varieties of these, from white to deep purple.

ERYTHRONIUMS. The type, *Erythronium dens-canis,* rose coloured and similar in appearance to a fine cyclamen, is only 6 in. high. Many of the new ones are much taller and have larger flowers. They include such varieties as Lilac Wonder, Purple King, Rose Queen, and the mixed hybrids produce a gorgeous variety.

These are pretty plants for the shady nook, for they like partial shade, a moist but porous soil which is well drained. This means plenty of humus! Dog's tooth violets are best left undisturbed.

GLADIOLI. Most early-flowering gladioli, unlike the larger forms, have to be planted in autumn and in most parts of the country they need some protection. They are best planted deep — 3 in. in rich soil — in autumn. It is advisable to cover the ground before the onset of winter with straw litter or chopped bracken which should be removed in March.

Gladiolus byzantinus is listed as a wild plant, and certainly it grows like a weed in some Somerset gardens I know. Recently I have introduced it into

The imposing crown imperial, *Fritillaria imperialis,* likes a rich but well-drained soil

my own garden. The species are *G. colvillei* and *G. nanus* and its varieties are all delightful and dainty.

Summer, Autumn and Winter

Since so much of the glory of our spring comes from flowers grown from bulbs, new gardeners are often unaware that many summer-, autumn- and even winter-flowering plants can also be grown in this simple way. To mention only a few, the lilies, gladioli and montbretia come from bulbs or corms. A small annual sum spent on unusual bulbs will bring interest, colour, joy and excitement a thousand times over.

Most summer-flowering bulbs should be planted from March to May and in the case of gladioli, chincherinchees and some others it is often best when planting several dozens to stagger the planting and put some in every fortnight so that the season is stretched. Plant the autumn-flowering kinds in late summer. Most summer-flowering types can be planted from the beginning of September to mid-December, lilies in autumn or in spring.

19

You will find more about these summer-flowering bulbs in the chapter on flowers for cutting. Among these summer flowers are some of the loveliest we grow. Many of them are from Africa and so are likely to be tender when grown in a colder climate.

AMARYLLIS. *Amaryllis belladonna*, the belladonna lily, is surely one of the most glorious of all late summer flowers. It is closely related to the hippeastrum, often called amaryllis, which is grown in pots on a window-sill.

The secret of growing the belladonna lily successfully is to find the right spot. Once these plants are established they will need little attention. The best site is a bed at the foot of a south wall where they can be left undisturbed.

Spend time on preparing the soil. Work in plenty of coarse sand, leafmould, manure (cow manure is said to be the best) or garden compost before planting.

If you live in a mild locality plant the bulbs so that their tips are just under 2 in. of soil. However, if you live in colder districts you would be wise to set them from 6 to 9 in. deep. Plant them well apart also, about 12 in.

The leaves appear first and then die down before the flowers which follow much later. Should the summer be a dry one, water the plants while they are growing. Every spring mulch the site with well-rotted manure or garden compost.

COLCHICUMS. *Colchicum autumnale*, the meadow saffron, is very variable and sends up distinctive large crocus-type flowers in white, pink, through lilac, carmine and purple. The large leaves follow in spring and often grow as tall as 18 in., so be sure to allow for this, not only when spacing the large bulbs, but also when planning the areas in which they are to grow. These bulbs are an exception to the general rule for in spite of their size they need only a shallow (2-in.) covering of soil.

They flower rapidly after planting, usually in August, but established plants are likely to begin flowering in late July. Be sure to plant them immediately on receipt or you may find them all in bloom in the bags!

The variety *C. a. major* flowers in September and October. Other species are available, including the purple *speciosum* which flowers from October to November and the yellow *C. luteum* which flowers in February.

As we might expect, the resourceful Dutch hybridists have been at work with colchicums and the hybrids now available are more robust than the species, which have weak stems and are inclined to flop about in bad weather. All are beautiful with large, even enormous, blooms and stems 6 to 8 in. tall.

CROCUSES. The true autumn crocuses are also quite delightful and easy to grow. Their soft purples look so well with autumn-tinted leaves and Michaelmas daisies. If you haven't grown any before, I think you will be delighted with the speed with which they appear and flower after planting. They are good for naturalizing so why not try some as a ground cover?

These true autumn crocuses have the typical grass-like foliage which appears before, and remains with the blooms. The centres of the flowers are gay, many having a lovely gold base to the petals and glorious orange-gold anthers.

The lavender-pink *Crocus zonatus* flowers first in September. Then follows *C. banaticus* and *C. speciosus*. *C. speciosus albus*, a lovely white form, and the scented *C. longiflorus* both flower from late September to October; while *C. speciosus globosus*, a lovely violet blue, flowers in November and December.

You will not often find these crocuses on shop counters. I advise you to order them early from a bulb merchant who catalogues them and who will send them to you as soon as the bulbs are imported.

IRISES. The Spanish and English irises are the earliest of the summer-flowering kinds, blooming in June.

The true Spanish iris is *Iris xiphium*; those you buy from your bulb merchant are its hybrids and varieties. You can buy them in separate colours or mixtures.

As far as I know, the English iris, *I. xiphioides*, its hybrids and varieties are always sold as mixtures. These bloom later than the Dutch and Spanish and, I think, more resemble the flags, with their beautifully velvety look. Colours are violet blue, purple, mauve and white, and some are prettily broken.

Both kinds like a well-drained, gritty soil. Plant in September and October. Lift and divide the bulbs after three years.

NERINES. When on one occasion I wrote about nerines my postbag was much heavier than usual. These beautiful flowers, sometimes called Guernsey lilies, are members of the amaryllis family. The individual florets, which are smaller than the belladonna lily's, are produced in large umbels sometimes with as many as twelve flowers. One other beautiful characteristic is the lustre, often like gold dust, on the petals.

Nerine bowdenii and its seedlings which bloom outdoors in September and October are really only hardy in mild areas, and even then they should be given a sheltered spot. Like the amaryllis, they like the foot of a south wall, although I have also seen them growing in a south-facing border backed by a fence. They can also be pot grown quite successfully.

Plant the bulbs from August to November, with the tip of the bulb just below ground level, in light sandy soil enriched with manure or garden compost. Topdress each August. Lift, divide and replant every four years. Do not expect much flower the year after planting.

Not all bulb merchants sell nerines and even those who do often only list the pink *N. bowdenii*,

but there are a few specialists, mostly lily growers, who have a larger range of the modern hybrids.

STERNBERGIA. Although crocus-like in appearance, *Sternbergia lutea* belongs, like the daffodils, to the amaryllis family, and is in fact sometimes known as the autumn daffodil. The flowers are only 4 to 6 in. tall but they are extremely distinctive. They appear in late September and October and are better the year following planting. They are also best left undisturbed.

LILIES. Today's lilies are truly a wonderful sight. During the past twenty years, hybridists have succeeded in extending the colour range of the different species so that, as well as the lovely pure white which most of us associate with these romantic flowers, we have also vivid carmine, butter yellow, buff, apricot, red, rose, green and mahogany, as well as a hundred subtle colour harmonies.

Most lilies are hardy but a few need to be grown in a greenhouse and a few others need to be protected from spring frosts when they are starting to grow. Generally speaking, they like their heads in the sun and their feet in the shade. Like us, they are not always happy in dull, wet summers. They seem

The showy pink heads of *Nerine bowdenii* are especially welcome in the autumn garden, but the plants require a sheltered spot and thrive only in milder areas

Lilium Enchantment, a Mid-century Hybrid with bright nasturtium-red flowers. The modern lily hybrids make a wonderful display

to grow best among shrubs where the soil around their roots can be left undisturbed.

The planting season depends upon the type of lily you wish to grow, for they are divided into two groups: those which produce roots only, where you would expect them, at the base of the bulb, and others which root first from the base of the bulb and later, as they grow, from the base of the stem also. The latter have to be planted much deeper, 8 to 10 in., than the base-rooting kinds which are best planted at a depth of 4 to 6 in.

These are general rules only and depend to a certain extent on your soil. In heavy soils, for example, it is best not to plant quite so deep but instead to topdress with good soil round the base of the stem as the plant grows. As always, there are a few exceptions! The delightful Madonna lily, *Lilium candidum*, is best planted with the top of the bulb just under the soil and the tall *L. giganteum*, now correctly called *Cardiocrinum giganteum*, which you would imagine would need to go very deep in order to be well anchored, should have the neck or nose of the bulb just out of the ground.

In the catalogues of lily specialists, you will find the various types clearly marked. Lilies, like the narcissi, are so varied and have been so hybridized that these also are now classified into defined divisions as follows:

DIVISION 1, the Asiatic hybrids; 2, the Martagon hybrids; 3, the Candidum hybrids; 4, the American hybrids, which means hybrids of American species; 5, the Longiflorum hybrids; 6, the Trumpet hybrids; 7, the Oriental hybrids; 8, all hybrids which have not already been classified in previous divisions;

and 9, all true species and their botanical forms.

Order your lily bulbs early and plant them as soon as they arrive. The species with basal roots always take longer to establish themselves. Some of mine did not appear at all during the first year after planting.

Mark the sites carefully so that you do not disturb them once they are planted and watch for weeds, removing the tiniest as soon as you see them so that you will not have to dig deeply to prise them out later.

Lilies which prefer acid soils seem also to enjoy the company of rhododendrons and heathers. These include *Lilium auratum, bolanderi, brownii, canadense, columbianum, grayi, japonicum, kelloggii, occidentale, pardalinum, parryi, parvum, rubellum, rubescens, superbum, wardii* and *washingtonianum.* If you have ordinary soil you can add peat or well-rotted leafmould. A mulch of cool leafmould or soaked sedge peat is helpful in summer and also keeps down weeds.

Others which tolerate lime and calcareous soils are: *L. amabile, brownii, bulbiferum croceum, candidum, carniolicum, chalcedonicum, dalhansonii, davidii, hansonii, henryi, leucanthum centifolium, maculatum,* Marhan, *martagon, monadelphum, pomponium, pumilum, pyrenaicum, regale, sargentiae, testaceum* and *tigrinum.*

Those that will get along well in ordinary garden soils are: *L. amabile,* Backhouse hybrids, *bulbiferum croceum, candidum, cernuum, chalcedonicum, dalhansonii, davidii, davidii* Maxwill, *davidii willmottiae, hansonii, henryi, maculatum,* Marhan, *martagon, monadelphum, pomponium, pyrenacium, regale, szovitsianum, testaceum* and *tigrinum.*

Take care of your lilies while they are growing. They enjoy a good drink in dry weather when they are growing fast. If you find that roses and any other plants in your garden are infested with greenfly then spray the lilies also as a precaution because the aphids can spread a lily virus disease.

Allow the old flower stem to remain on the plant until its leaves have turned faded and yellow — because while these are green they are still working to make a new bulb for next season's flowers.

Many lilies produce tiny bulblets on the portion of stem which is underground and some even produce them on the portion which is growing above the soil. You can carefully remove these young bulbs and grow them on in a little nursery bed until they are large enough to plant elsewhere.

Flowers from Tubers

A tuber differs botanically from a bulb or a corm in that it is really an underground stem with buds — for instance, a potato and its 'eyes'. Tubers which are cultivated in the same way as bulbs and corms usually are catalogued by bulb merchants under the general heading of 'bulbs', but it is as well to know the difference between them because this may influence certain points in their cultivation, such as lifting and propagating.

Tuberous-rooted plants are not so sharply divided from other plants as those which grow from bulbs or corms. Sometimes the root stock or rhizome of a plant is swollen and tuber- or bulb-like and can be lifted and treated in the same way. So don't be surprised or confused if you find a well-known plant, such as hardy geranium or oxalis, popping up in a bulb catalogue.

Generally speaking, tubers listed in bulb catalogues are not perfectly hardy in all areas and if you have any doubts at all it is advisable to lift them and store them in some frost-proof place for the winter. Alternatively, some may be pot grown.

ANEMONES. Some anemones are grown from tubers, while others, such as *Anemone japonica*, are bought as perennials. Among the former are the cheerful poppy anemones, *A. coronaria*. You will find more about these in Chapter 12, 'Flowers for Cutting.'

As well as these excellent cutting flowers, there are other anemones which are well worth growing, indeed I cannot imagine spring without them! *A. blanda atrocaerulea* is one of the bluest of our little spring flowers. There are also other forms of *blanda* in white, pink and rose. These flower from January onwards, according to the season and the locality. Also a beautiful blue is *A. apennina* which comes into bloom with the cherry blossom and will spread a sky-matching carpet beneath if you plant the tubers thickly enough and leave the plants undisturbed so that they can increase. Of breathtaking brilliance is the single scarlet *A. fulgens* which blooms in April. Like the poppy anemone, this species is also good for cutting.

All tuberous anemones need a moderately light soil which has been liberally charged with well-rotted leafmould, garden compost, manure, peat or some other good humus-providing substance.

BEGONIAS. Surely begonias must be acknowledged as being among the most gorgeous of all summer bedding plants. As richly coloured and often as beautifully shaped, they can take the place of roses in beds and situations where these

23

The large-flowered tuberous begonias with their glowing, rich colours are among the most highly decorative of all the plants for summer bedding

shrubs would not thrive or look well. Although they grow and are highly decorative in beds, begonias are also splendid container plants. I have mentioned them in my chapter on seeds and pot plants.

The cheapest and in some ways the most fascinating way of raising these begonias is from seed, and the knowledge that the plants thus raised will then produce tubers which can be kept for another year is pleasant. I discuss these plants in more detail in the next chapter. For plants which are to be raised from tubers, the easiest method for outdoor cultivation is simply to plant the tubers in the beds or container in May, and by the time the leaves are appearing above the soil all fear of frost should be past. However, the most satisfactory method and one which ensures earlier flowers is to start growing the tubers in March. Space them out in shallow boxes of light, rich potting compost. If you mix your own, use one part each of good loam and well-rotted leafmould (or failing this, of peat) and half a part of clean, coarse sand. Just press the tubers down in this mixture so that they are almost covered. They need a temperature of 16 to 18 °C. (60 to 65 °F.) and should be kept moist but not wet.

If you have no greenhouse you can use a cold frame, a shed or some similar place, perhaps even a windowsill in a garage or in a spare room. In any case this must be frost free and in good light and well ventilated by day. Cover them with clear plastic to keep them humid until growth begins. When the roots begin to grow and the little leaves begin to appear on the surface of the tuber, transplant them to deeper boxes to give each tuber more room. You can also use individual pots.

Once the tubers start growing in the moist compost, take care when you are watering them if they are exposed to sunshine. See that you do not drop water on the young leaves or they may become scorched and brown.

Do not plant the begonias outside until the frosts are over. They do best in rich soil and partial shade. If you wish to save them for another year, lift the plants in September or before the frosts, place them in boxes to ripen off and allow the foliage gradually to die down, then when this has completely faded, clean the tubers and store them in a cool but frost-free and dry place until you are ready to start them again in the spring.

CANNA. Every year an aquaintance of mine has a colourful and amusing display of flowers growing all along one side of a building in her garden. The display is colourful because the plants are cannas, with handsome dark-coloured leaves and bright yellow and red flowers. They amuse me because they are always grown in old oil cans. In spite of the ordinariness of the containers the plants put on a brave display.

The best I have ever seen were growing in

beds along the busy main road in Mâcon, France. These really were very splendid indeed. The roots, usually sold as tubers but really portions of rhizomes, should be grown on in exactly the same way as begonias, except that instead of being spaced out in boxes they should be potted. By the end of April they can be moved outdoors to a cold frame. They should not be planted in the open until early June or at such time as the frosts are past.

Before the frosts in autumn the plants should be lifted and put, quite close together, into boxes filled with ordinary soil. They should then be kept nearly dry and stored in a dry, frost-free place until potting time comes round again.

ERANTHIS. One of the gayest of spring carpets in my own garden is provided free – by the masses of wild celandines which I have allowed to remain in certain parts. These are glorious in their season and little trouble later for the only signs of them from summer onwards are the clusters of tiny tubers. Not everyone has a garden large enough to be able to allow wild flowers to have their way, but I mention them here because I am reminded of them by the winter aconites or eranthis which belong to the same family. Only 3 to 4 in. high, they have the same golden freshness, the same gleam to the petals. They are distinguished though by a dog-Toby collar of green just below the petals which protects them when they are in bud.

They will grow in any ordinary soil and almost anywhere, except in really dry situations, but I think that they look their best carpeting the ground under trees. They will grow also on rock gardens, in beds, and in shady borders. Good all-rounders, in fact. In lawns you will find that they are not a nuisance because the foliage disappears quite early in the season, so don't cut it down, and always leave them undisturbed, wherever they are.

Eranthis hyemalis blooms earliest, followed by *E. cilicica,* which is a little larger and has slightly bronzed foliage. *E. tubergeniana* is twice as large as *hyemalis* and, a nice bonus, it is also fragrant.

Plant the little tubers as soon as possible after they become available.

If you plant several of each species rather than a mass of one kind you will prolong the flowering season. If you have the space and care to plant a mixture of winter aconites, species crocus, snowdrops and scillas you will have a charming piece of garden embroidery just when flowers are scarcest.

RANUNCULUSES. Closely related to the anemones are the ranunculuses – double, multi-coloured buttercups, a friend of mine calls them – which give wonderful flowers for very little trouble. I used to grow these in rows for cutting but I now like them in little groups in the foreground of shrubs and other plants.

They like a well-drained soil and a sunny situation and you can plant the tubers from February to May, according to the season and the district. You will find the little tubers are like dried claws; always plant them with the claws pointing downwards. Various species and varieties are available.

GERANIUM. Unexpectedly, perhaps, among the tuberous plants is the little geranium (not to be confused with the pot geraniums which are really pelargoniums), *Geranium tuberosum.* This has 9-in.-tall, large, purple-violet flowers, little crane's bills, which appear in May and June. It is an attractive plant for a rock garden where it will sprawl nicely in a sun-warmed place.

DAHLIAS (see also Chapter 12, Flowers for Cutting). You can buy dahlia tubers from seedsmen or bulb merchants and from garden centres or stores. To get early flowers it is best to plant the tubers in pots or boxes of soil in a frost-proof greenhouse or frame and get them growing well. They should not be planted out in the garden until June for they are easily damaged by frosts. A few weeks before they are to be planted out gradually harden them. The best way to do this is to stand the pots out during the day and take them in at night in case of frost.

Alternatively, the tubers can be planted where they are to flower. This can be done from early May onwards. If the tubers start into growth quickly and the shoots are well above ground before all danger of frost has passed watch for forecasts and protect them with straw, polythene, newspaper or some suitable covering.

I have grown dahlias in this way, and although they flower later than those grown from plants this method is quite satisfactory in good seasons. But if the spring is late and cold I have found that the tubers fail to grow.

SALVIAS. One of the loveliest of blue flowers, the 3-ft.-tall *Salvia patens* grows gracefully in a border but it is not hardy. You can also grow it in a greenhouse. The tubers should be started in heat in March and grown on until June when they can be planted out in ordinary but rich or enriched soil. Lift the tubers in October, dry and store them in sand in a frost-proof place.

Flowers from Seed

Annuals are plants which have a brief though glorious life; biennials differ from them because they are sown one year to flower the next and then die, and perennials go on living for many years. Most can, of course, be raised from seed although it is more usual for the last to be increased by division or from cuttings.

Most flowering plants increase themselves from seed but there are many reasons why not all flowers form seed and also why some seed will not germinate. Quite often, weather conditions are not suitable for ripening the seed. It may be that the correct insect or some other animal by which the flower's pollen is spread does not exist in the area and that there is no substitute, which means that the seed is infertile.

Some seed needs to be sown as soon as it is ripe, which means that such a seed could not be packeted in the usual manner. On the other hand some seed will not germinate until it has been kept some time and vernalized – which means subjected to low temperatures (frost). Many berries need to be vernalized by being buried between layers of sand in a pot and kept outdoors throughout the winter. They are then more likely to germinate if they are sown in the spring.

This is not the whole story for I have tried to make it as simple as possible, but even from these few observations you can see that it is not as easy as it may seem to save your own seed.

Only species come true from seed, so when it is possible to save seed of such plants you can expect to see the same flower appear. You should not, therefore, be disappointed if the seed you save of varieties, or hybrids, produces flowers which do not truly resemble the parent plant.

You will see that some novelties are described as F_1 hybrids. These hybrids will never come true to seed which you try to save yourself. The reason why F_1 seed is dearer than other kinds is that the cross between the two selected parents (the first cross, hence the name), has to be made anew each season.

For all these reasons, I always think it is a false economy to try to save seed. Even if the seed was right in the first place one needs to know a great deal about storage, why some seed loses its vigour and why age does not seem to affect other types.

But, on the other hand, there is a way of saving seed which is usually satisfactory because it is the natural way. Certain plants in a garden will seed themselves. Weeds do this a little too efficiently! But certain garden plants do so also and whether or not you want to encourage, or even allow, this will depend upon the type of garden you have.

If you have formal bedding schemes and lift plants as soon as they are shabby to make way for something else, it is unlikely that you will find plants of the same kind appearing on their own the following year. Also, if you are careful to dead-head all large annuals, you are not likely to have self-sown plants. But there are some plants which are not easily kept tidy, nor would it be desirable — forget-me-nots and sweet alyssum are examples. Here you have a flowering stem still producing blooms at the tip while at the base of the stem seed is already ripening. So, inevitably, many seeds are dropped and unless removed when young will grow just as their parents did.

So far as the two flowers I have mentioned are concerned, this is of no consequence, because the type flower is often quite good enough. But you will also find that where you have bought a special strain, say Excelsior foxgloves, and allowed the plants to drop their seed, you will see in time that the foxgloves have reverted back to the type and are no longer the special strain.

The same happens with poppies, double nasturtiums and many other flowers. If you prefer the variety, your remedy is not to allow the flowers to seed and to sow bought seed freshly each year. Otherwise you can save time and money by allowing the plants to grow naturally.

In my own garden I compromise. For ground cover, forget-me-nots and alyssum are allowed to seed where they grow. Often, if I want a drift of the same flowers under some shrubs elsewhere, I lift some seeding plants and heel them in or even just cast them on the ground where they can drop their seed. Later, the shabby old plants are removed. Some honesty, dame's rocket, foxgloves and poppies are allowed to seed where tall plants are needed. Sweet Williams, wallflowers, nasturtiums and violas are a few of the others which are allowed to grow naturally — but, as I said earlier, I have plenty of space for them.

On the other hand, I continually raise new plants from new seed. This adds interest to the garden as well as giving me something to look forward to.

I imagine that even the newest gardener realizes that it is possible to raise gay flowering plants easily from seed when these plants are annuals, but I don't think it is generally realized how many other plants may be raised in the same way. It really depends on how much time and patience you have. Money isn't so important in this case because it really is so much cheaper to raise perennials and certain (but by no means all) shrubs, climbers and other plants from seed.

While daffodils, tulips, irises and other large-flowered bulbs should have their faded blooms removed, crocuses, chionodoxa, scillas and other low-growing small flowers should be allowed to make seed so that they will become naturalized.

Many border plants, both annuals and perennials, can be easily raised from seed. This border includes plantings of nicotianas, antirrhinums, border carnations, verbenas, petunias and asters

In this case the little seedling bulbs do not take long to produce a flower, tiny though it may be, to add to the general effect.

However, it may take as long as five or seven years to flower a daffodil or other large bloom from seed. Some lilies, *Lilium regale* in particular, will flower from seed in two years, so this is well worth trying. Others take longer. As I said earlier, it depends on your time and patience!

I have species lilacs (these have more feathery flower clusters and a sweeter scent than the hybrid lilacs), philadelphus or mock orange, roses, leycesteria, cotoneasters and tree lupins all from seed, as well as many perennials and climbers such as the pretty eccremocarpus and clematis.

If you are moving house and beginning a new garden, it is well worth while making both a cold frame and a nursery bed right away so that you can have something growing ready for the time when the garden is landscaped.

You will find that most seed firms list many biennials and perennials in extremely reasonably priced packets. One firm, quite unique (I believe it is the only firm in the world to do so), issues a very full and comprehensive catalogue of many kinds of plants obtainable from seed. This is Thompson and Morgan Ltd. of Ipswich. As these seedsmen are careful to point out in the catalogue, some perennial plants, particularly alpines, present more difficulty. But if at first you concentrate on the less finicky herbaceous perennials you should be well rewarded.

Bear in mind that while some seeds germinate very quickly, some others, usually the choicer alpines, remain dormant for as long as two years. This is one reason why choice seeds are sown in seed pots or pans, which can be kept and inspected from time to time.

The best time to sow seed of hardy perennials and shrubs is from the end of March, through April and May. A cold house or cold frame is best. These plants do not need artificial heat.

You can use the John Innes seed soil mixture, a soilless compost or make your own mixture of 2 parts good loam (this is best sterilized), 1 part peat or well-rotted leafmould, and 1 part coarse, clean sand. To each bushel of the mixture add $1\frac{1}{2}$ oz. superphosphate. For all except lime haters, add $\frac{3}{4}$ oz. garden chalk.

I favour the use of clean plastic bags. Place each seed pan in a bag, inflate this and fasten it tightly at the top, tie on the label, put it in the frame and you can forget it until the seeds germinate. Open the bag when you can see the true leaf appearing between the seed leaves. When this is well grown lift out the little plants carefully so as not to break the roots and pot them individually or plant them out 3 in. apart each way in a little nursery bed. Move again when they have outgrown this space – to their permanent homes, if this is convenient.

If you need bedding plants, then there is no doubt that the cheapest way to obtain them is to raise them from seed yourself. I have no greenhouse yet each year I manage to raise many kinds by using the wide, sunny window-sills in my country cottage. Each year I raise something new, simply because I am interested to see just what can be grown in this way. So far I have found that all those which are said to need a greenhouse can also be grown in the home, so long as you have the space. Once the seedlings are growing well they can be moved out to frames, to window-sills in a garage or shed, or if they are not very tender plants, to wait their planting time under cloches.

Naturally if you have a greenhouse there are many more plants which you can grow simply because there is more space at your disposal.

One feels that if a gardener has the facilities to grow his own plants he would be wise to grow those which are not usually to be found on sale. This involves a study of current seed catalogues. Some gardeners like to grow a novelty each year. I had one dear friend who always looked for the most colourful and bizarre flowers to plant in the beds in front of his house 'to startle the natives'. He enjoyed seeing the people of the tiny village where he lived walking by on a Sunday evening to gaze at his display.

I think that new gardeners might be inhibited by the very glory of some plants into thinking that to raise them would be beyond their skills, but this is not likely to be so. Take begonias, which I have already mentioned. These are easily raised from seed. There are both tuberous and fibrous-rooted kinds. The latter, known as *Begonia semperflorens*, are covered with a mass of small flowers and are ideal also for containers of all kinds including individual pots. They flower until the frosts arrive. They should be sown early in the year during January and February and then grown on so that they have become sturdy little plants by early summer when they can be planted outdoors.

It is customary, and certainly space saving, to

prick off seedlings into boxes, but for my part I prefer to pot them individually. Plants knocked from pots suffer much less of a check than those prised from boxes. But it is possible nowadays to buy boxes which are divided into sections, which act in much the same way as small pots. However, if one is counting pennies the less money one has to spend on these items the better. I use a great many of the black plastic bag type, possibly expendable though I tend to save many of them from year to year. If I have reason to believe that the plants will be waiting for a long period before being planted out I fill the bag-pot almost to the rim, but most of the time I turn the top down and use just half its depth, which is about 2 in. This is usually deep enough for most seedlings and one finds that by using this method there is a great saving in seed compost.

To return to the begonias. Seed hybridists have raised some most attractive varieties in recent years. Some, such as the Super Danica, have large flowers some 2 to $2\frac{1}{2}$ in. across and attractive bronze-red leaves, handsome plants indeed and easily raised from seed.

Pelargoniums, usually called geraniums, are certainly well worth raising, especially now that there are new, early, free-flowering types. If the seed is sown early, in January or February, the plants will be ready for bedding at the usual time. One, an F_1 hybrid called Sprinter, is a good red and dwarfer than any other pelargonium raised from seed. If you like an assortment of colours, Carefree Mixed, also an F_1 hybrid, should suit you.

All the half-hardy annuals usually seen on sale are worth raising from seed. However, those which are known as half-hardy annuals are not always so botanically but are so called for convenience. They may actually be biennials or perennials, but because they are half hardy it is more convenient to treat them as annuals.

Among these are the snapdragons or antirrhinums, half-hardy perennials. Here there is a wonderful range for the enterprising gardener. For my own part I like the old-fashioned snapdragons, and among these the most wonderful are the tall, 3-ft. varieties which look so distinctive when growing among other plants in a border. There are also low antirrhinums, ideal for those whose gardens are in the path of the winds, or for clothing rock gardens quickly and cheaply. There are double-flowered varieties, penstemon-flowered and bell-flowered, of many hues including

Pelargoniums for bedding purposes are well worth raising from seed. Enclosed in a border of white alyssum is the variegated-leaved variety Caroline Schmidt

white. The secret with antirrhinums is to sow the seed early in spring so that they make sturdy little plants by the time they are to be set out. Pinch out the centres when the seedlings are a few inches high to encourage them to become bushy.

Other worthwhile hardy annuals and perennials are certain carnations, especially the perennial Chabaud Special Mixture, which has large, double, romantic-looking flowers in white, yellow, pale pink and on through the rose hues to crimson. In mild districts these plants will live through the winter. Enfant de Nice will flower in five months from an early spring sowing. The flowers are big and blowsy, some $2\frac{1}{2}$ to 3 in. across, and among the white, red, rose and salmon will be some which are engagingly striped. Both these varieties are sweetly scented.

Other dianthus, known as annual pinks, are also

well worth growing. This year I have raised (on the window-sill) the new hybrid novelty Magic Charms. The plants are only 6 to 8 in. high and are smothered with single flowers some $1\frac{1}{2}$ in. across. They make mats of colour and are just the thing for border edgings or for flat gardens on stone and for planting among paving in patios.

Plants I find extremely satisfying and well worth raising from seed are the dusty millers, *Cineraria maritima*, half-hardy perennials. These will live through mild winters or will survive in mild areas. Any gardener will be glad to have a couple of dozen of these plants at his disposal, for they are useful among dark-foliaged plants to emphasize the richness of their colours. They help fill in spaces in grey or silver borders. They grow extremely well in containers of all kinds, where they harmonize beautifully with the customary container plants such as pelargoniums and petunias, heliotrope and begonias.

Dahlias are often overlooked as plants one can raise from seed, yet if these are sown early they will flower the same year and at so little cost. The plants make tubers as they grow and these can be lifted and saved. As you might guess, it is mixtures of various hybrids that are sold. I suggest that the gardener does his own selection, marking and saving those which particularly appeal and discarding the remainder should these not be so attractive or prove unsuitable in some way.

If delphiniums, which are really hardy perennials, are treated as half-hardy annuals, they can be used to bring a little extra and unexpected colour into the autumn scene, for if you sow the seeds early in spring, then pot and grow the plants on in individual pots, moving them on to larger pots whenever this is necessary, planting them out in May or June and watering them well should the season be dry, you will get fine spikes of flowers in the autumn. One gardener I know grows these in pots but keeps them in a cold frame. He lets them flower, and keeps only those most appealing to him. He then cuts off the young flower spike once he has seen its colour, because he says that by doing this he gets a better show of spikes the following year.

Apart from these few I have mentioned, there are so many perennials, biennials, trees and shrubs which are easily raised from seed, and seed itself is so cheap, that I am inclined to be philosophic about it and say that should harm befall your seedlings and you come through with only two or three plants, you will still have shown a profit.

Some of the most satisfying plants which I have raised from seed have been those which have handsome and distinctive foliage. I have already mentioned the silver-leaved cineraria but there are others, more hardy perennials of greatly contrasting shapes, size and textures. Some are evergreen, or at least winter-worthy, others die down each year. These include such handsome plants as hostas, ligularia, phormium, a group of which would look splendid in themselves; acanthus, euphorbias and hellebores such as *Helleborus corsicus* and *H. sternii*, which combine unusual and long-lasting inflorescences with striking foliage; the marble-leaved, low-growing, hardy cyclamen, the glorious meconopsis, the woolly silver-leaved lamb's ear or stachys, which can be contrasted in shape and style by the wonderful metallic, spiny-leaved *Eryngium delaroux* and the pretty lady's mantle or alchemilla, which has charming lobed, grey-green foliage and masses of foamy yellow-green flowers which are lovely for cutting and which also dry well.

With the expenditure of a few pence and a little time one can soon furnish a garden distinctively and at the same time create a source of continual pleasure. One of the nice things about raising seed in pans and boxes is that it provides a pleasant task for those times when one feels up to only a little gentle pottering, or perhaps when the weather is not clement enough for other forms of more active gardening.

It is usual to sow perennials outdoors in late spring or early summer and then to thin them out, transplanting them to a nursery bed where they can grow uncrowded until they can be moved to their permanent quarters. In the early days when our cottage patch was a haven for slugs and snails, I found that I lost too many plants when growing them this way and so I made a custom of sowing the perennial and biennial seed in boxes and then pricking the plants off into individual pots large enough to sustain them while they grew into plants sturdy enough to go into their permanent quarters. I still use this method, simply because I find it so convenient. The time for thinning and transplanting seedlings grown in the nursery bed so often comes both in very dry weather and at a time when one is busy picking and preserving fruit. When grown in boxes I can begin to prick off the seedlings as soon as they have made one or two true leaves. I stand the pots in rows down the side of the path in the vegetable garden where they are under constant inspection. This way I can daily select the plants which are ready and plant them out two or three at a time. Conducted this way there is not the same urgency about raising the plants.

I should perhaps remark here that not all perennial seed germinates as quickly and freely as annual seed. Some, like shrubs and trees, will not move until they have been vernalized, or subjected to frost.

Among the biennials there are many beautiful, old fashioned, endearing plants such as Canterbury bells and honesty, Sweet Williams, wallflowers and other cheiranthus to scent the air, cynoglossum, which resemble forget-me-nots, and forget-me-nots themselves, which incidentally come in pink as well as blue; foxgloves whose leaves when young are ideal for covering the ground and which will grow handsomely under trees and in the shade, although they will also grace open borders prettily; Brompton or winter stocks, hardy and floriferous, which bring a summer scent to spring gardens, and the lovely, silver-downy *Verbascum bombyciferum* for silver borders or for planting to contrast the lovely blues of delphiniums and hardy geraniums.

Among the most decorative of all foliage plants are two common vegetables, cabbage and kale, sometimes listed as Decorative, sometimes Flowering, the latter name really not apt because the only flowering they do is to produce the usual soft primrose coloured brassica flowers. These are quite sweet, but it is for the plants' leaves that we grow them. The foliage is white, cream and amethyst in various tints, shades and hues, usually variegated. When in heart the cabbages are like giant roses sessile on the ground. The kales make taller plants and I always grow some in my mainly silver border where the soft colours of their leaves mingle beautifully with the grey and silver plants. They are especially beautiful in early spring.

For those who like distinctive plants, annuals both hardy and half hardy will provide a great diversity. As I said earlier, a seed catalogue will prove to be a treasure chest. But while searching for the new I like also to hold fast to the old. In my view my own garden would not be complete without some familiar friends, poppies, love-in-a-

The silver-downed leaves of *Verbascum bombyciferum* make a pleasing foil for the brighter colours of other perennials and are of especial value in the silver border

mist, night-scented stock, candytuft, Virginian stock, mignonette, linaria, alyssum and marigolds for instance. Some are sown in September and these grow on through the winter, flowering early in the summer. As a general rule hardy annuals do not flower for such a long period as the half hardies, and there comes a point when, even though they are still producing blooms, the plants are so ungainly or untidy that they are best pulled out. March sowings will produce flowers late in the summer. After this date, if you have the space, I think that it is worth growing them in just the same way that one grows annual vegetables, in succession. Rather than sow all the seed at one time, make an early sowing in March and then sow a pinch or so as each new batch of seedlings appears above the soil. This is a good way of keeping filled the odd seasonal gaps which occur in borders. Annuals treated this way should still be in flower at the end of autumn.

There are many lovely climbers which can be grown from seed, some for temporary decoration and others much more permanent. Of the first, and par excellence, are the sweet peas. Modern varieties which produce long-stemmed flowers each with many florets are so easy to grow. Each year, and for cutting, I grow Galaxy varieties all along the west side of a large cage which covers and surrounds my vegetable garden. The plants climb the wire netting of which the sides are formed. They receive little attention beyond an occasional feed and watering, and of course the constant picking of the flowers, a most pleasant chore!

There are other annual climbers. The tall, easy-to-grow nasturtiums for instance will soon cover a screen and give masses of blooms, doing well and flowering best on poor soil. One climber, sold as a half hardy, is really a perennial. This is *Cobaea scandens*, the astonishingly beautiful cup-and-saucer flower, which if it is given a warm and sheltered spot will come up year after year as it did when I once grew it on a roof garden in London. Among the true half-hardy annuals are the ipomoeas. Heavenly Blue is a perfect name for one variety and there are other colours.

There are also many hardy perennial garden climbers which can be raised from seed, the popular wisteria being an example. Not that you are ever likely to need all the plants you might get from one packet of seed, but surpluses can always be passed on as gifts, or you might like to try your

hand at bonsai (the Japanese art of dwarfing trees), for which several of the climbers are suitable.

Other hardy climbers include *Campsis radicans*, clematis, both the species and mixed hybrids, *Eccremocarpus scaber* and *Lathyrus latifolius*, the everlasting pea, crimson and rose, the white form of which, White Pearl, is very lovely indeed.

Most gardeners find seedlings of shrubs which have grown from seeds which have been 'bird-sown', but it seems to me that few of them think of raising shrubs and trees for themselves. As you would expect, some take many years to flower, but others come into bloom in what seems a remarkably short time. Azaleas, for instance, will bloom only three years after sowing.

Some germinate like any other seeds and often almost as quickly, although one should be prepared for a little delay. Some of those which are easy include azalea, cistus, erica, hypericum, buddleia and pieris.

Others might take twelve months, even after stratification (immersing the berries in sand and allowing them to freeze). Many in fact need to be stratified before they will germinate and usually the seedsman will indicate which these are. As these are, in the main, the most numerous, I suggest that when in doubt it is best to sow all seeds of trees and shrubs in this way. Sow the seed in pans or boxes in January. Excavate a little garden soil to make a depression to take the containers, so that their rims are just flush with the soil surface. Let them remain in this situation throughout the winter for about six to eight weeks. Then bring them indoors to greenhouse, frame or even living room, wherever the temperature can be kept to about 15 to 16°C. (60°F.). Keep the pans moist and shaded. I would recommend that at this point the individual containers are enveloped in plastic bags.

If you know mice to be troublesome in the garden, securely cover the seed boxes and pans with wire netting.

Some flowering shrubs and trees which can be raised from seed, apart from those already mentioned, are: abutilon, akebia, arbutus, berberis, carpenteria, caryopteris, ceanothus, ceratostigma, cercis, chaenomeles, cornus, cytisus, daphne, fremontia, genista, hibiscus, *Hydrangea villosa*, kalmia, kolkwitzia, lavandula, leycesteria, lonicera, magnolia, mahonia, malus, osmanthus, paeonia, paulownia, philadelphus, rhododendron, rosmarinus, viburnum and wisteria.

Flowers from Shrubs and Trees

When you think of a rose bush in full bloom or a laburnum tree festooned with golden chains you can appreciate that shrubs and trees can be as colourful as any annual or other herbaceous plant. Few of them have as long a flowering season although roses seem to become more and more perpetual blooming as the years go by, but it is possible, with a little planning, to have some flowers the year round.

Of course, whether or not you have flowers during the bleakest days will depend upon the locality of your garden as well as on the severity of the winter. Suitable plants are described in Chapter 8, 'Flowers for Winter'. But even if the weather is cruel, so long as you have some plants that would under better conditions produce flowers, you can cut some branches from them to open in the warmth of your living room (see page 87).

Fortunately, many of the shrubs and small trees are very floriferous in their seasons. If some are also evergreen, like the lovely camellias, or if the flowers are followed by berries, or beautiful autumnal foliage or pretty fruits, like pyracanthas or the ornamental crab apples, you have a bonus!

Not many of those which flower in winter are flamboyant (although a wall covered with winter jasmine is as pretty as anything you could see), but what many lack in show they make up for in fragrance. Witch hazels, and their near relatives, corylopsis, viburnums, and winter sweet or chimonanthus are all really fragrant. They bloom during the darkest days of the year and are thus doubly sweet. The cherry family, prunus, has members which begin flowering in October and will blossom on all through the winter until spring, so long as the flowers are not killed by really severe conditions.

The more sheltered the place you can give these winter-flowering types, the better they will do. This is one reason why you often see shrubs which are not true climbers planted near the walls of a house. You can read more about these in Chapter 7, 'Flowers for Special Places'.

Spring and early summer do not offer much of a problem since so many of the familiar shrubs and small trees flower then, but readers often ask for advice on plants which blossom in August and later. One of the shrubs in my own garden which gives me greatest pleasure is leycesteria, sometimes called Himalayan honeysuckle, sometimes flowering nutmeg. It has pendant clusters of wine-red

Left: Shrubs and trees can be as colourful as any perennial plant. Included in this mixed shrub border are hypericum, fuchsia, a deep purple hebe, senecio and hydrangea, with the golden-leaved *Robinia* Frisia in the background. The bulbous flowers in the foreground are tigridias

Top: Shrub roses make an excellent informal hedge. This is a fine example of the old-fashioned variety *Rosa gallica versicolor*

Bottom: *Clematis* The President growing through *Elaeagnus pungens aureo-variegata*. The beautiful large-flowered clematises are invaluable for covering a wall or for use as screening plants

bracts studded with little white flowers which are very beautiful and the half-woody stems remain green and attractive throughout winter. Mine grows on a north border and gets larger every year. The birds have obligingly cast the wine-red berries in other parts of the garden where other self-sown plants are growing.

The tree mallow (*Lavatera arborea*), which has small hollyhock-like flowers of various colours, blooms from August to September and there are several hardy fuchsias well worth including in a border.

Hydrangeas are more varied than you might suppose. *Hydrangea macrophylla* is the kind you buy in a pot from the florist. This, incidentally, may be planted out in the garden where it will grow into a large plant in time, but you may find that it will change considerably in colour, according to the mineral content of the soil, for hydrangeas prefer an acid or peaty soil. One of the best ways to ensure that your hydrangeas keep a good colour is to maintain a generous mulch of peat around the plants. Blue varieties can be made bluer by using hydrangea colourant, which can be bought at garden stores.

Many people plant hydrangeas near the porch, or in some other place in full sun, which is a pity because in hot summers the colours are bleached. A partially shady position would be better. Although most hydrangeas, including the beautiful lacecaps, prefer a peaty soil there are species that grow well on non-peaty soils. Here, obligingly, the white kinds grow whiter so these are worth selecting. *Hydrangea paniculata*, with pointed, lilac-shaped clusters of flowers, makes a handsome plant.

The pretty ceratostigma, only a foot high at first, but gradually making a spreading bush some 3 ft. through, flowers from June to the very end of autumn, its leaves turning a deeper and deeper wine colour contrasting well with the sky-blue flowers. It favours a position at the foot of a wall.

The size of your garden should always influence your choice. There are so many neatly sized trees and shrubs that it would be a pity for you to choose one which grows so large that it has to be cruelly cut. There are many misapprehensions about cutting trees and shrubs. Most of them grow far better and bloom much more freely if they are left alone. Look around you when you go into the country in spring and see how well the wild shrubs and trees bloom with no one to prune them!

If you are in doubt do not prune at all. Merely cut away any dead, dying or obviously weakly shoot as near to the main stem or perhaps to the ground as possible. The reason that one prunes or cuts growth from a plant is two-fold. We may need to keep the plant well shaped or under control and we also want to induce it to give many flowers of high quality. Some unpruned bushes produce plenty of bloom but it is often small; this may suit your purpose in which case the plant can be left to grow naturally.

Not all shrubs produce flowers in the same way. Some produce their flowers on the new shoots which have grown from nice fat buds earlier in the year — hydrangeas, roses and buddleias are examples. Obviously the thing to do is to coax them to make many good fat buds. Strangely, we do this by shortening the old stem in spring and even though we cut away several inches of stem which obviously has buds on it we get more blooms from the few buds that remain on the short stem, even if these are no more than 'eyes'. All the effort that the plant would have used in nurturing all the buds — some of which are almost certain to have been blind — is now spent on the remaining few.

Some shrubs flower on shoots made the year before, long enough ago for the soft growth to become woody, and so we say that the shoots are produced on the previous year's wood. Conveniently for us, most of these flower in the spring and where required we have to cut them back or prune them after they have bloomed, so that the lower and dormant buds can get busy and produce lovely long shoots of green in plenty of time to turn woody, ripen and make flower buds for the following spring's blossom. Often, merely cutting branches for flower arrangement is sufficient pruning. Be selective and cut crossing, twisted or weak stems.

Many evergreens grow well and flower well with no pruning at all. Should one grow too large for your garden cut it back some time at the end of May, but only if you are quite sure that all danger of frost is past. If not, wait a little longer. Instead of cutting away bits and branches from various parts of the bush, which could be harmful and which in any case will give you an unnatural looking plant, take out one branch right to the base. This way you really do make the bush smaller, it occupies much less space and the remaining portion can go on growing naturally.

If any evergreens, like camellias, become badly

A prostrate broom with creamy-white flowers, *Cytisus kewensis* is a shrub of great decorative value. It looks well in a corner of the rock garden

damaged by severe frosts do not prune the frosted part until late May, then cut away all the frosted portion until sound wood is reached. Try to find a dormant bud and cut back to that.

Some shrubs do better if the seed heads are removed as soon as possible. Rhododendrons and lilac in particular will flower much better if this is scrupulously done.

If you have old lilac trees which have become straggly and bare low down and do not flower well, cut them right back really severely after flowering. In three years you will have bushy trees again.

As I said earlier, one of the great advantages of growing shrubs is that if you have enough there will always be something to delight and interest you. At first you can plant quite closely and remove or even discard some when they tend to crowd each other. Or you may prefer to fill the spaces between those which will grow large with smaller, even ground-carpeting shrubs. It is possible also to make mixed borders. Bulbous plants and shrubs grow well together and if you include those which flower in autumn as well as spring bulbs you will help to strengthen the year-round flow of colour which should be our aim. And of course you

can use perennials and annuals, either as groups between the shrubs or as ground covers. If you do this, select the kinds carefully, because some grow so large or gross that they may smother the shrubs. On the other hand, such plants as alyssum, lobelia and tiny tagetes, usually seen in formal bedding or in containers, can often be used as ground covers. They can look very lovely grown in this informal manner.

Shrubs and trees grow in such a variety of ways that it is possible to find some for every purpose. Sprawlers play an important role, to cover ground, to soften and furnish paving, to fill in portions of a rock garden, or even to cascade over a wall. These include *Cotoneaster conspicua decora, C. microphyllus, Cytisus kewensis,* junipers and other evergreens such as the shrubby herbs like thyme and prostrate rosemary, low-growing hebes and of course ivies, of which there are many which are attractively coloured.

Opposite left: A delightful blue-flowered shrub is the ceanothus, seen here trained against a wall and intermingled with the orange-flowered climber *Eccremocarpus scaber.* In the foreground is *Choisya ternata*

Left: Both ribes, the flowering currant, and the cheerful yellow perennial doronicum, so useful as ground cover, thrive in an alkaline soil

Bottom: For a moist, shady situation hostas are good ground-covering plants. Here the cream-margined leaves of *Hosta crispula* set off well the pink fronds of *Astilbe simplicifolia*

It is both surprising and gratifying to discover just how much colour one can get from a mixture of shrubs and small trees. One attractive area in my own garden at the moment includes a purple-leaved maple tree, a grey-leaved *Cytisus beanii* smothered with yellow, lupin-like flowers, golden privet and a golden and a blue conifer.

Many herbs look well in shrub borders. Some of the salvias or sages are truly lovely, *Salvia officinalis purpurescens* and its multi-coloured form, for instance. Rue, or *Ruta graveolens* Jackman's Blue, really does look blue on some days. There are lavenders in variety from the dwarf, neat and very floriferous Twickle Purple to the tall, sweetly perfumed English lavender.

If you have only a little garden, or if you want to pack in as many flowers as possible, you can introduce a great deal more colour by using flowering plants as hedges. These, incidentally, are also often less work because they do not need regular clipping.

Probably the most popular type of hedge of this kind is one of roses. Many of the hardy, vigorous modern floribundas are perfect for this purpose. We must not forget either that a flowering floribunda hedge is a continuous source of flowers for the home for many months of the year.

There are also many other types of roses that make good outer hedges, and a keen rosarian would on request present you with a considerable list of roses, species, hybrids and varieties which would certainly be suitable for a hedge. But not all are labour saving for the weekend gardener and certainly not all are suitable for a small garden. It is one thing to remove dead wood or to thin out in March, but another also to have to remove limitless dead flowers during summer, a time when so much else calls for attention. On the other hand a rose hedge does bring an indefinable something to a garden.

The old-fashioned roses, under which heading all but the modern hybrid teas, polyantha and floribunda roses go, do not flower for such a long season as the others, but make amends by having beautifully showy fruits (rose heps) in the late summer. Many of the low-growing species and varieties make charming little hedges. The Fairy or Perpetual Miniature rose listed by seedsmen can be raised from seed. The flowers are mostly single and mainly pale pink, not very showy, but quite endearing. They flower in summer from seed sown in pans in spring but they take several

years to grow dense. But many of the other smaller varieties also do well grown in this way. *R. chinensis*, Baby Crimson, 2½ ft.; Baby Masquerade, 1 ft.; Cécile Brunner, 3 to 4 ft. and Perle d'Or, 2½ to 3 ft.; *Rosa sempervirens*, 2 to 3 ft. will all give colour right through summer and on into the autumn. These small plants need very little attention and put up with a chalky soil better than their taller and larger cousins.

A walk around a nursery which specialises in these roses should prove revealing and entertaining. Listed on page 44 are a few of the proven types of hedge roses.

Many of the vigorous-growing modern roses make splendid plant screens, dense in summer but light in winter. Among these are Peace, Frensham, Queen Elizabeth and Masquerade. These will grow from 4 to 8 ft. Plant them 2½ ft. apart.

Floribundas may be cut constantly while in flower and while cutting a fresh rose it is not really difficult nor time absorbing to reach out and remove a faded one. This constant cutting is in itself a form of light pruning and induces the production of new flowering stems. In fact it can be all that is given, but generally the plants will respond better if they are given a slightly harder pruning in the spring.

There are some other roses which also call for little work and they are listed later.

A rose hedge looks charming in association with some other plant growing as a low hedge before and below it. A good choice is a plant which retains its leaves all winter so that when the rose bushes are bare of foliage, as they are in winter, there will be some other plant to hold the interest. I recommend the silver or grey-leaved shrubs such as lavender, santolina or senecio, all of which will contrast so prettily with the young red-bronze shoots of rose in the early spring. If these silver bushes are allowed to bloom there is the extra value of summer colour. Sometimes tall-growing roses are planted with a dwarfer form before them which according to variety will form a hedge from about 18 in. to 3½ ft. high.

There are many other suitable plants. If I were on acid soil and had a sheltered garden I would make a hedge of slow-growing camellias. Think how lovely that would look!

A friend of mine has a chaenomeles hedge and the bright red flowers are a joy in spring. She gathers the fruits (quinces) for pies and jellies. The dainty deutzia, weigela, erica, escallonia (good for seaside gardens), forsythia and fuchsia (think of those holiday hedges in Devon and in Ireland) are all suitable hedge shrubs.

Some friends of mine in Derbyshire have planted a hedge of hebe, sometimes called veronica, all around the boundary outside their garden wall. Always evergreen, in summer it is a mass of purple and very lovely. This strikes me as being a really charming social act, since they themselves can see it only when they are outside their own plot.

The pretty orange kerria, lavender (try making a hedge of mauve, white, purple and pink mixed), myrtle, if you are in a sheltered district; olearia, osmarea, philadelphus or mock orange, potentilla, ribes or flowering currant, spiraea and viburnum are just a few others. In fact the concept of a flowering hedge is of sufficient importance to be considered seriously when planning a garden from scratch. Bear in mind that none of the subjects mentioned is a clipped hedge in the accepted meaning of the term, but I should like to repeat a point made earlier, that cutting for flower decoration

Deutzia, with flowers which include lovely shades of pink as well as white, makes an attractive informal hedge, flowering in early summer

can often take the place of pruning. Take for example forsythia. If branches are cut in bud for forcing and again later when almost in bloom, less pruning will be needed later.

Informal hedges are seldom narrow and all tend to spread and grow in width, so do not entertain the idea of any informal hedge unless a width of at least 3 ft. can be allowed.

Many of these informal hedges or plant screens are composed of deciduous plants and consequently they will be really dense in summer only, but even without leaves once they become established they will make good screens.

If garden room is scarce such screens can sometimes be made to be productive. Cob and filbert nuts, which produce attractive catkins in spring, can be grown, especially on stony ground. They can be planted as closely as 3 ft. and will grow as high as 10 ft.

One should remember that once planted a hedge is normally there for life and so the soil should be well prepared, enriched and deeply dug. The ground should be fed again in the second spring after planting with some long-lasting fertilizer such as bonemeal. A mulch of well-rotted animal manure or home-made garden compost applied at intervals over the years will keep the plants in good heart.

Bottom: Planted as a single specimen in the lawn a flowering tree such as this graceful weeping cherry, *Prunus subhirtella pendula*, is a source of pleasure at every season and especially at flowering time

Opposite: The mixed blues of delphinium varieties with a foreground of lavender create a delightfully soothing effect. Delphiniums are a good choice for an acid soil. In the left foreground is *Santolina neapolitana*

Nurserymen usually sell hedging plants at the 100 rate, which is less expensive than buying them individually. Young plants should be spaced so that they will touch, or almost do so, a year after planting. They should not be allowed to race upwards, but sides and tops should be trimmed so that in the early stages a thick base is formed. Once this is achieved the hedge can be allowed to grow upwards and outwards as desired, but try always to keep the top narrower than the base if you are ever likely to get heavy snows which might break branches.

Informal Hedge Plants

Apples and pears, providing both blossom and fruit, can be grown as pyramids and planted 3 to 3½ ft. apart. Prune the short side branches in order to keep the centre trunk thick.

Also worth growing are:

Amelanchier ovalis and *integrifolia* (snowy mespilus)
Berberis thunbergii and *B. t. atropurpurea*
Cornus mas (cornelian cherry)
Cotoneaster lactea
Cytisus albus (white Spanish broom)
Deutzia rosea
Forsythia intermedia and varieties
Kerria japonica
Osmarea burkwoodii
Philadelphus in variety (mock orange)
Poncirus trifoliata (golden apple)
Prunus cerasifera in variety
Prunus triloba flore pleno
Pyracantha rogersiana and varieties
Rhododendron luteum (also called *R. flavum* or *Azalea pontica*)
Rhododendron ponticum (common rhododendron)
Ribes sanguineum (flowering currant)
Spiraea menziesii
S. vanhouttei
Symphoricarpos rivularis (snowberry)
Weigela florida (bush honeysuckle)

Informal Hedges that do well in Seaside Gardens

Berberis darwinii
B. stenophylla
B. buxifolia
Buddleia globosa
Choisya ternata
Cotoneaster in variety
Escallonia virgata
Fuchsia magellanica riccartonii

Griselinia littoralis
Hebe speciosa, many varieties
Hippophae rhamnoides. Plant one male to eight females.
Lonicera pileata yunnanensis
Olearia haastii

Low Formal Hedges Between 2 and 4 ft.

Caryopteris clandonensis
Ceratostigma willmottianum
Erica mediterranea
Hypericum patulum
Philadelphus Manteau d'Hermine (mock orange)
Potentilla fruticosa (cinquefoil)
Spiraea thunbergii
Viburnum opulus compactum

Low Formal Hedges Suitable for Seaside Gardens

Hebe cupressoides and *H. traversii*
Lavandula spica, L. vera (old English and old Dutch lavenders)
Myrtus communis and *M. c. tarentina* (myrtle)
Rosmarinus officinalis (rosemary)
Hydrangea macrophylla, H. grandiflora and *H. paniculata*

Hedges Under 2 ft. in Height

Berberis thunbergii atropurpurea nana
Hyssopus officinalis (hyssop)
Lavandula spica nana and varieties (dwarf lavender)
Ruta graveolens (rue)

Hedges Under 2 ft. Suitable for Seaside Gardens

Berberis buxifolia nana
Lavandula
Santolina chamaecyparissus (lavender cotton)
S. c. nana
Hebe anomala

Rose Hedges

Rosa alba hybrids (such as Celestial, Maiden's Blush and the Jacobite rose)
R. borboniana hybrids (Bourbon roses, such as Zéphirine Drouhin and Kathleen Harrop, both thornless)
R. chinensis (the China rose)
R. eglanteria (the sweet briar, sometimes called *R. rubiginosa*)
R. moschata (musk rose, varieties such as Penelope)
R. rugosa hybrids (such as Pink Grootendorst)
R. xanthina (Canary Bird)

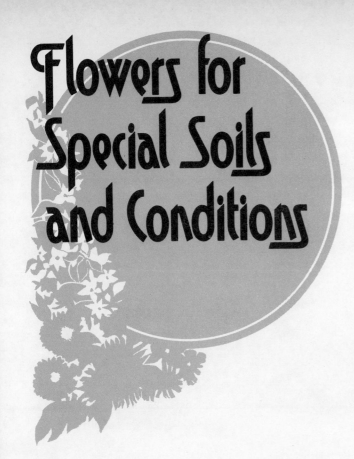

Flowers for Special Soils and Conditions

Fortunately, the majority of flowers will grow on or in ordinary soils better than on other kinds. But where special soils do exist it is important to grow the plants suited to them rather than to try to adapt the soil to the plants.

I do not intend to go too deeply here into the nature of all the different soils and it should be sufficient to say that, generally, they are either acid or peaty, or limy or chalky. In between falls the great mass of ordinary soil which is neutral or almost neutral, though it may be poor and need enriching. This quite often can be simply adjusted to take acid-loving plants by mixing in and mulching with peat. Even quantities of home-made garden compost will help to turn neutral or almost neutral soil acid. Alternatively, one can add lime in its various forms (all neatly and conveniently packed nowadays) to make a neutral soil more limy. What you cannot do is to make a limy soil acid simply by adding peat. It is also a waste of time to dig a deep hole and fill it with peat for some acid-loving plant because, inevitably, rain water will bring in more lime from the surrounding ground. The only thing to do is to make a raised bank of the acid soil. Nor can you make a peaty soil limy enough to grow the true chalk lovers. So you have to compromise.

A local nurseryman will give you guidance and so will a study of wild plants around you. If foxgloves grow wild freely, you are on acid soil. If beech trees fill the woods you are on chalk or lime. If you are uncertain of your soil (and by the way it *can* vary from the top of the garden to the bottom) you can either test it yourself with a simple-to-use kit bought from the chemist or garden shop or, alternatively, send various samples taken from several spots in the garden (a trowel full from each is enough) to a garden chemist or to your local horticultural adviser.

Many plants normally associated with peaty soils (these are known as calcifuges) have members of the same family that will tolerate a certain amount of lime in the soil. Ericas, or heaths, are an example of this. In our limy-soil garden, we have built a mound which we call our peat hill on which many calcifuges flourish well above the normal ground level. Lower down, at a point where roots are bound to be affected by the lime, we have planted those ericas which we know will tolerate it. These are the *Erica carnea* varieties and they have grown there for over ten years now and continue to flourish.

Left: A rock and pavement garden provides the opportunity to grow many delightful ground-hugging plants, such as the sweet-scented thyme, saxifrages and alpine phlox

Top: Forget-me-nots and low-growing heaths have been effectively used as ground cover in this lovely corner — the perfect foil for the delicate colouring of *Rhododendron augustinii* at the back of the border

But be warned, don't attempt to grow in really chalky soil any plant which is said to be just tolerant of lime. Chalk holds just too much!

When he was a little boy our son asked if he could have a magnolia, so we bought him *Magnolia soulangiana* which we knew would tolerate a certain amount of lime. We planted it on level soil and used peat liberally among the roots, spreading more over the soil in a deep mulch. When, after a few months, the leaves appeared to be more yellow than green, we gave it a dose of sequestrene, a substance which helps calcifuges take iron from limy soils, something they seem unable to do naturally. We could see the effect of the chemical in twenty-four hours for the leaves next day were already turning a deeper green round the margins. Our boy's magnolia is now some fifteen years old and is growing slowly and surely. It receives an annual quota of sequestrene and an early summer mulch of peat and lawn mowings, as do so many other plants in the garden.

Do remember that peaty soils are rich with humus – this is what makes them acid – but that limy soils are often deficient in it so the more humus you work into it the more neutral it will become.

The superb *Magnolia soulangiana* with its goblet-shaped, wine-tinged flowers, prefers an acid soil but will tolerate some lime, especially if regularly mulched with peat

Although the peaty soils allow you to grow the glorious rhododendrons and azaleas and other members of the erica family, you will find that there are many shrubs and trees which flourish on chalk and lime and will give you lovely spring blossom and autumn colour.

More herbaceous plants seem to be more lime tolerant than shrubs and, generally speaking, these are easier to accommodate since their roots do not penetrate so far. In the section on lilies in Chapter 1, 'Flowers from Bulbs and Corms', you will find a selection of lime lovers and haters.

Heavy soils are the greatest trial, for they are hard to work and cold and wet for the plants. In this case it is best to concentrate on individual sites and make all planting holes larger than they should be so that they can be lined with peat and/or leafmould and a liberal amount of sand. But there are plants that will tolerate heavy soils, camellias and day lilies (hemerocallis), in particular.

Sandy soils at least are well drained, and slugs are not the nuisance that they are on heavy soils. But they are often very poor and should have plenty of humus added to them. While you are improving the soil so that choicer plants may be brought in, you can have a good show from brooms, barberries, hypericums, lavenders and rosemary (in fact most grey-leaved plants do well in sand) and all kinds of bulbous plants.

Near the sea and in hilly districts, you find the problem of gardens situated on a dry slope which, especially if they are grassed, become parched and starved. One of the best ways of dealing with such a garden is to plant it with shrubs which, in time, because of their own leaf-fall and the annual mulching they should receive of manure, compost or peat, will enrich the soil. One should spend a little time and money on enriching the soil before planting begins. Peat and leafmould will quickly introduce essential humus. Bonemeal is slow acting and so will be present in the soil ready to be taken up by the plant once growth is active.

Certain other plants, not only herbaceous ground coverers but little bulbs also, can be grown beneath and between the shrubs.

In some districts, near industrial towns, it becomes difficult to grow certain plants because they succumb to the polluted atmosphere. On the other hand it is well known that roses grown in such districts are free from black spot, a fungus disease. However, if you have had failures, replanting may be the answer.

Hardy Perennials that will Thrive in Alkaline Soil

Aconitum (monk's hood)
Allium (onion flower)
Alyssum
Anchusa
Anemone
Aquilegia (columbine)
Artemisia (wormwood)
Campanula (bellflower)
Catananche
Dianthus (pinks)
Doronicum (leopard's bane)
Echinops (globe thistle)
Erigeron
Euphorbia (spurge)
Gaillardia
Geranium (cranesbill)
Gypsophila
Helleborus (Christmas and Lenten rose)
Hypericum (St John's wort)
Iris
Lathyrus (everlasting pea)
Lavandula (lavender)
Linaria (toadflax)
Nepeta (catmint)
Paeonia
Papaver (poppy)
Pulmonaria (lungwort)
Saponaria (soapwort)
Scabiosa (scabious)
Tradescantia (spiderwort)
Verbascum (mullein)
Veronica

Flowering Trees, Shrubs and Climbers for Alkaline Soil

Aesculus (horse chestnut)
Aucuba
Azara
Berberis (not *thunbergii* and its varieties)
Buddleia
Cercis (Judas tree)
Chaenomeles (quince or japonica)
Choisya (Mexican orange flower)
Cistus (rock rose)
Clematis
Clerodendrum
Cornus (dogwood)
Cotoneaster
Crataegus (thorn)
Deutzia
Erica carnea

E. darleyensis
E. mediterranea
E. stricta
Escallonia
Euonymus europaeus
Forsythia
Hibiscus (tree hollyhock)
Hypericum
Laburnum
Laurel
Ligustrum (privet)
Magnolia kobus
Malus (flowering crab)
Philadelphus (mock orange blossom)
Potentilla

Papaver orientalis Mrs Perry, a salmon-pink variety of the oriental poppy. It thrives best in an alkaline soil

Prunus (flowering cherry, almond, etc.)
Ribes (flowering currant)
Senecio
Sorbus (mountain ash and whitebeam)
Spiraea
Symphoricarpos (snowball tree)
Syringa (lilac)
Veronica
Viburnum
Weigela (diervilla)

Hardy Perennials that will Thrive in Acid Soils
Agapanthus
Alchemilla
Amaryllis
Anemone
Aster
Astrantia (masterwort)
Boltonia
Caltha (marsh marigold)
Cephalaria (giant scabious)
Chrysanthemum
Coreopsis
Crinum
Cyclamen
Delphinium
Dicentra (bleeding heart)
Epimedium (barrenwort)
Eremurus
Ferns (in variety)
Gentian
Geum
Gillenia
Helenium
Heliopsis
Hosta (plantain lily)
Kniphofia (red hot poker)
Liatris (blazing star, gay feather)
Lilium auratum, brownii, humboldtii, speciosum
  and some other species
Lupin
Lychnis (campion)
Meconopsis (blue poppy)
Monarda (bee balm)
Nerine
Physalis (Chinese lantern)
Phlox
Physostegia (obedient plant)
Primulas
Pulmonaria (lungwort)
Rudbeckia (cone flower)
Sternbergia

Trollius
Vinca

Trees, Shrubs and Climbers for Acid Soils
Acer (maple)
Andromeda
Amelanchier
Arbutus (strawberry tree)
Azalea
Berberis thunbergii and its varieties
Callicarpa
Calluna (ling)
Camellia
Clethra (white alder)
Cytisus (broom)
Daboecia (Irish heath)
Erica (heather)
Eucryphia
Fothergilla
Hamamelis (witch hazel)
Hydrangea
Kalmia
Magnolia
Parrotia
Pernettya
Rhododendron
Skimmia
Rosa rugosa varieties
Viburnum dentatum

Flowering Trees and Shrubs for Poor, Sandy Soil in Dry, Sunny Sites
Berberis
Campsis (climber)
Caragana
Colutea (bladder senna)
Cistus (rock rose)
Cotinus coggygria (smoke bush)
Cytisus (broom)
Genista
Hebe (veronica)
Helianthemum (sun rose)
Hypericums
Jasminum beesianum
Lavandula (lavender)
Phlomis fruticosa (Jerusalem sage)
Robinia
Santolina (lavender cotton)
Spartium (Spanish broom)

Perennials for Dry Shade
Anaphalis margaritacea (pearly everlasting)

Aquilegia vulgaris (columbine)
Asperula cynanchica (woodruff)
Bergenia, in variety
Campanula latifolia and C. trachelium (bellflower)
Digitalis purpurea (foxglove)
Epimedium alpinum (bishop's hat)
Geranium, in variety
Hepatica americana, syn. Anemone hepatica
Hypericum androsaemum (tutsan), H. calycinum
  (rose of Sharon)
Lamium maculatum and varieties (dead nettle)
Liatris in variety (blazing star)
Mertensia in variety
Monarda in variety (bee balm)
Pachysandra procumbens and variegata
Polygonum affine
Pulmonaria in variety (lungwort)
Saxifraga umbrosa (London pride)
Symphytum officinale (comfrey)
Vinca in variety (periwinkle)

Perennials for Moist Shade
Ajuga reptans and varieties (bugle)
Anemone in variety
Dicentra spectabilis (bleeding heart)
Ferns in variety
Geranium in variety
Helleborus in variety (Christmas and Lenten
  roses)
Hosta in variety
Lysimachia nummularia (Creeping Jenny)
Oxalis acetosella (wood sorrel)
Podophyllum in variety
Primulas in variety
Pulmonaria in variety. Tolerant.
Saxifraga in variety. Tolerant of many shade
  conditions.
Solidago in variety (golden rod)
Tiarella cordifolia (foam flower)

Perennial Ground Cover Plants
FOR SUNNY PLACES
Alchemilla mollis (lady's mantle)
Anaphalis triplinervis
Aubrieta, in variety (rock cress)
Centaurea dealbata (knapweed)
Frankenia thymifolia
Geum in variety
Hemerocallis in variety (day lilies)
Mazus reptans
Polygonum affine
Phlox subulata (moss pink)

Stachys lanata and varieties (lamb's ear).

FOR SUNNY BANKS
Heuchera in variety (alum root)
Iberis sempervirens (winter candytuft)
Nepeta in variety (catmint)

FOR SUN OR LIGHT SHADE
Aquilegia in variety (columbine)
Dianthus in variety (pinks)
Heucherella alba and tiarelloides
Hosta in variety (plantain lily)
Monarda, in variety (bee balm)
Mentha in variety (mint)
Prunella vulgaris laciniata (selfheal)
Vinca in variety (periwinkle)

FOR PARTIAL SHADE
Ajuga reptans and varieties
Bergenia in variety
Convallaria majalis (lily of the valley)
Saxifraga oppositifolia latina
Saxifraga umbrosa (London pride). Versatile.

Flowering Trees and Shrubs for Towns and Industrial districts
Ailanthus (tree of heaven)
Chaenomeles (flowering quince, japonica)
Cotoneaster
Crataegus carrierei
Deutzia
Escallonia
Forsythia
Hypericum (rose of Sharon)
Jasminum
Kerria (jew's mallow)
Koelreuteria
Laburnum
Mahonia aquifolium
Malus (flowering crab)
Neillia
Olearia haastii
Osmarea
Philadelphus
Prunus
Robinia
Rosa
Sambucus
Skimmia
Viburnum opulus
V. tinus
Yucca

Flowers for Special Roles

Many flowers can be used in a variety of ways to serve the gardener and help to create a pretty garden. They can be used as carpets, to suppress weeds as well as keeping the ground moist and prettily covered. They can be spread like mats on the ground in paved areas to add colour and also to perfume the air when they are trodden underfoot. They can be used as screens, canopies, drapes, camouflage, hedges, edgings and boundaries.

I use some plants, I call them my pioneer plants, to pave the way for other choicer kinds. Making my own garden has been no easy task because the area is surrounded by wild countryside and however hard we strive there are always plants that we don't welcome trying to get in and succeeding! To keep these out I let certain garden plants go their own way in a newly cleared patch until I have time to attend to it and plant it in detail. I have mentioned some of these, the biennials, in Chapter 3, 'Flowers from Seed', but I also use some perennials, such as golden rod, achillea, montbretia, arabis and stonecrops.

The most useful have been the dwarf Michaelmas daisies. In some cases I have let them cover square yards of border thus keeping it tidy most of the time and bringing lovely colour in the autumn. It has always been quite easy to dig out an area and enrich it when we have been ready to plant a shrub or tree. When new perennials have to be planted I find it best to clear a really wide area and to move the daisies on to some other site. If they are not wanted for replanting they can safely be killed while growing by using Weedol, after which the soil is quite all right for new planting.

One of the most useful roles plants can play is to decorate and cover the ground closely so that they prevent weeds from growing. Some ground covers can be very gay. In one or two places in my own garden, including an area at the edge of our rose bed, we let Creeping Jenny grow. The graceful trails of bright green leaves hug the ground covering it completely and then suddenly the plant is covered with starry yellow blooms which go on for weeks. A golden variety gives even brighter colour — and I have a friend who grows it in her garden where it covers square yards of soil mingling with rose-coloured stonecrop and sedums.

Because I have to be away from my garden such a lot I have gradually introduced many kinds of carpeting plants among shrubs, some of which I have mentioned in previous chapters. I recommend

A colony of *Helleborus corsicus*, a species of hellebore with pale green flowers, covering the shady ground under trees

this kind of gardening if you too have a large area which you want to keep as tidy in appearance as possible.

In the spring the tall golden daisies of doronicum, sometimes called leopard's bane, grow in a great mass below the greengage and other trees. These play a vital role in preventing weed seeds from germinating early in the year. The plant itself almost disappears once the flowers have faded but it's still there ready to come up again next spring. In summer I mulch the area with well-rotted compost, for this feeds the roots and also keeps down weeds.

The loveliest and bravest colour in my garden in spring comes, I think, from the complementary harmony of the purple honesty flowers and the yellow narcissi. The honesty looks after itself. I leave most of the plants in the borders so that they can seed and shine out in the winter gloom. But even the stems which are picked and dried for winter decoration contribute plenty of seed as

the outer seed cases are being peeled off. This is taken and scattered on various parts of the borders.

At last, in one part now deep and humusy I have managed to get the hellebores or Christmas and Lenten roses established. Since these are native to my part of the country I am hoping that they will colonize themselves. In smaller gardens you may need flowers which take a little less room. Suitable ones are tiarella, lily of the valley, variegated dead nettle, *Ajuga tricolor*, heartsease, alchemilla, violets, celandines, and periwinkles, all of which grow in my own garden. The familiar and endearing London pride (*Saxifraga umbrosa*) will also grow nicely over the ground.

But of course not all ground to be covered is shady or moist or both. Quite often there are sunny, dry, even arid places which need covering. These too can be flower-filled areas for you if you choose your plants carefully.

Many of the little pinks or dianthus are good for this purpose. The maiden pink, *Dianthus deltoides*, has bright pink flowers – quite small – on 6-in., wiry stems. What they lack in size they make up for in quality for the plant will make a neat mat of foliage which will become almost hidden by bloom. If you begin by planting closely you can expect a mass of colour through the summer.

53

This is also a good pink to plant between paving stones. There are several forms (one, Wisley Variety, with rich bronze leaves) and a mixture planted will look most attractive.

Although perennial plants are mostly used as ground covers it is also possible to use certain low-growing annuals and I feel that this is a practice that might appeal most to those gardeners who like to make a clean start each autumn. I have already described how I use the annual sweet alyssum as a ground cover in my mainly silver border where it seeds itself. If you have an area in the foreground of shrubs you might like to consider growing annually some of the coloured alyssums as a sweet-scented ground cover to help keep down the weeds during summer. Pink Heather, Royal Carpet and the taller Lilac Queen are all very pretty varieties which will look particularly attractive with silver-grey shrubs or roses.

The Busy Lizzie, or impatiens, is also a good garden annual which does especially well in a moist, shady spot. Colours are varied and a packet of mixed seed gives some fascinating results, really brightening an area of ground. If you prefer one kind, Kirchrot is very vivid. Blaze is a lovely velvety rosy red. F_1 Imp Deep Orange is outstanding. These are just a few varieties which have impressed me recently. The fibrous-rooted flowering begonias, also raised as annuals from seed, would do well in a similar situation.

Lobelia, really perennial but treated as an annual, is another plant which deserves to be grown in some other way than alternated with alyssum or pelargoniums in a garish bedding scheme. One of the prettiest ways I saw recently was a long, narrow edging bed on each side of a path leading to the front door of a house; the bed was completely filled with *Lobelia* String of Pearls. This is a pretty mixture containing many soft, subtle colours.

Recently, under some cherry trees long past their blossom time and thick with foliage, I saw a great mass of dwarf nasturtiums. The combination of fresh green foliage and vivid flowers was very lovely and since these particular plants flower best in poor soil they did not seem to mind sharing the site with the greedy cherries. There are many dwarf-growing annuals which may appeal to you for use in this manner for both sunny and shady sites.

One of my most vivid memories of a beautiful garden path will always be of one leading to the front door of a house in Surrey. Made of crazy paving it offered a happy home to sun roses and fragrant little pinks of all kinds. Here and there mat-forming thymes hugged the stone and came to no harm when they were trodden upon. Instead they sweetened the air with their summery scent.

I like to use thymes to cover large areas of ground. Indeed, at the moment I am planning to cover a new pathway with a combination of paving stones and thyme. I am taking cuttings from the many kinds of creeping thymes I have for this purpose. Not only are these plants evergreen but they become smothered with flower in summer. Bees visit them and when one treads on the leaves the pungent sweet scent is released to delight one's sense of smell.

You can soften areas of any kind of stone by using the ground-hugging plants. Often a path, courtyard or a drive needs this treatment. Try making the edges of your concrete paths prettier by planting soft, grey-leaved plants and allow them, here and there, to trespass a good way on to the surface. Use the pretty little Cheddar pink, *Dianthus caesius*, *deltoides* and its varieties, and, for lime-free soil, the 3-in.-high *D. neglectus*.

Friends of mine who have a garden in Derbyshire in a locality where there exists only a thin layer of soil on the underlying rocks, have made a delightful garden by concentrating on the many pretty stonecrops and flat-growing rock plants and carpeting kinds. There is no lawn but every square inch of ground seems to be covered and the garden is always full of interest and, at times, it is a carpet of bright colour.

The stonecrops or sedums are well worth studying for they are beautiful as well as easy to grow. Apart from the prettiness of the flowers, the plants are lovely and decorative in themselves, some more so than others, as you would expect. One of my favourites is the little *Sedum spathulifolium* Cappablanca. The leaves grow in little rose-like clusters and are a light silvery grey and covered with a meal or bloom. The flowers are similar to those of the wild yellow stonecrop which I also grow. The plant is as decorative without flowers as it is in bloom. I grow it in many ways, to fill crevices among paving, in tufa stone, in the corners of sink gardens, at the rims of containers holding mixed plants and even in the foreground on my mainly silver border. Like all these plants it is

Small plants inserted between the stones soften a paved area or path. Some of the ground-hugging plants, such as thyme, scent the air when the leaves are trodden on

easy to propagate; one just pulls off a little rosette with a few roots adhering.

A lovely rosy-hued favourite is *S. cauticola* with fleshy leaves tipped with the same hue. Ruby Glow, with purple-grey foliage, is also handsome. Its stems are 9 in. long but not high, for this plant has a lax, flopping habit which is not offensive, as the stems cover the ground nicely. Some sedums die down in winter. Of these the showy *S. spectabile*, the ice plant, 1½ ft. tall, is perhaps the best known. Its large flat heads of massed tiny pink flowers bloom late in summer. Butterflies are attracted to them. Also late flowering is *S. spectabile* Autumn Joy, whose stems and leaves become plum coloured – an attractive variety of a native plant.

In a group not far from the house I have a collection of various types of terra-cotta containers holding a very diverse collection of plants including a large seed pan, (planted with the beautiful little *Sempervivum arachnoideum*) and the tall chimney

which once rose from our cottage roof. Now instead of smoke this holds a feathery topknot of curry plant, while another chimney pot gives a home to silvery senecios. Among these and other pots I have a strawberry or crocus pot, fitted with pockets over its surface. These are all filled with sedums and sempervivums.

The latter, known as houseleeks, are also quite fascinating and well worth collecting. Once again, the plants themselves are beautiful – more consistently so, in fact, than the sedums. The rosettes of some species and their varieties resemble chunky green or coloured water lilies. The little one I referred to earlier is known as the cobweb houseleek because of the fine hairs which smother the little rosettes. It bears clusters of rosy-pink-purple blooms, which are often as large individually as the leaf rosettes. There are many others, all with distinctive, often strangely beautiful, flowers.

One of the great advantages of both these kinds of plants is that they will grow so well in any porous soil as well as in rock gardens. They will also grow well on the top of walls so long as you can provide a root hold of some kind. Indeed by using a double wall you could make a little border at an easy-to-work level and at the same time set aside a place to build up an unusual collection. You could soon furnish the top in a pretty way and once they reach the edges the plants will begin to drape themselves attractively over the side. If you would like them to cover the entire wall, you would need either to make a few pockets to take the roots or you might find it sufficient to use the spaces between the stones. If you build the wall yourself you could allow for this and even plant them as you go.

Many of the rock plants will grow in a wall like this. It is up to you to decide whether you want to grow plants which would appear to raise the height of the wall, rock roses for instance, or whether you would prefer to have plants which cling close to the stone. These include some of the pretty little speedwells, creeping phlox, campanulas or bellflowers. Mixed with those I have already described they could provide interest all the year round.

Like the sedums and sempervivums, campanulas vary considerably and it seems to me that I am always coming across new ones. There are so many species of annuals, biennials, perennials, plants for beds, borders, informal and wild gardens, rock and sink gardens, paving, even greenhouses, that I suggest that it might be best to choose your plants from garden centre or nursery unless you find them well described in a catalogue.

A species splendid for draping a wall is one with a frightful name, *Campanula portenschlagiana*, synonym *C. muralis*. Recently I bought a little plant of *C. rotundifolia*, the tiny harebell just 3 to 4 in. high. Walk round a rock garden nursery and you are sure to find several little charmers.

There are many thymes which will grow nicely over the edges as well as carpeting the top of a wall. They are evergreen and they become absolutely smothered with scented flowers which last for weeks.

If you are a busy housewife, with not very much time for leisure or to 'stand and stare', I would urge you to plant a 'kitchen sink' tree. Study the view from your kitchen window and plant the tree where it can best be seen from the spot where you seem to spend a large part of the day. This can be your very own tree: you will get to know it so well. You will be able to watch its progress each day while you are going about the mundane chores. You will find yourself waiting and watching for it to bloom and for its leaves to open in spring. You will see it slowly turn colour in the autumn or maybe even to fruit, depending upon what kind you

choose. In the winter you will be able to see its etched beauty against the sky – some trees have such lovely silhouettes.

It is important, though, that you are discreet in your choice and that you do not choose any tree which is going to grow so large that it will ultimately become a nuisance to you and your neighbours alike. Remember that large trees also have large root systems and under certain circumstances searching roots can gravely undermine the foundations of a house, so for a small garden choose a small tree. Remember, too, that a tree which will grow fast will also grow very large. It is much better to spend a little more in the first place on a really good specimen of a slower growing type.

Judging by the number I see growing, it is evident that the favourite tree of many new house owners is not a flowering tree but a weeping willow. This is frequently the first thing to be planted in a new garden and often it is planted so near to the new house that I shudder to think of the trouble it is likely to cause in the future. Apart from anything else, it will have to be sadly lopped. The weeping willow is not a tree for a small garden. It should be given plenty of space so that it can grow naturally and gracefully.

However, since I am confining myself to flowering plants in this book, and having given this warning, I can suggest other attractive trees which are pendant. In my own garden I have the neat little willow-leaved pear, *Pyrus salicifolia*, which has silvery leaves borne on graceful stems and in the spring these are studded with clusters of miniature pear blossom. There are some lovely weeping cherries. If you like catkins – these come with the leaves – a weeping birch can prove delightful. Some of the sorbus family have a slightly weeping outline and are neat and attractive trees. The mountain ash is well known but there are others. *Sorbus hupehensis*, the pink form, has pretty grey-green fern like leaves, slender branches and clusters of white, pink-tinged berries which birds don't like. The foliage turns a purple red in the autumn.

A magnolia is a delightful specimen tree and there are several varieties from which you can choose. Unusual and very lovely is the Judas tree, or *Cercis siliquastrum*, whose branches are studded with rosy-purple pea flowers in April before the leaves appear. It grows to an attractive shape. If you like white blossom and if you like to see

The rosy-purple pea flowers of *Cercis siliquastrum*, the lovely Judas tree, bloom in April before the leaves appear

berries on a tree – and the birds who are almost certain to come and eat them – the simple white hawthorn will give you a delightful tree to look at on any day. The berries are quite safe, should you have children in the family.

If you would like to marry usefulness with beauty, you could choose an apple, peach, pear or any fruit which takes your fancy.

Finding so few trees in our plot we were reluctant to cut down the ancient apples, even though they were neglected and somewhat diseased. More intense cultivation around them and the increase in the number of birds in the garden have helped to improve the trees. They always redeem them-

selves in spring by the marvellous show of blossom they produce, but for the rest of the year they are not highly ornamental. For this reason we have made them hosts to a variety of climbers.

There is the early-flowering *Clematis macropetala* on the tree nearest the house, a Dorothy Perkins rose, once on the cottage wall, at the end of the garden, an Albertine rose on an old plum, and more modern climbers on other apples, a climbing hydrangea, a honeysuckle, a wild clematis. After a while the climbers reach high in the branches and the trees appear almost to blossom again at another time of the year.

The *Solanum jasminoides* we have planted against the wall of the cottage has done so well, proving that it likes our soil, that I intend planting another specimen against one of the empty trees. I think that it should do very well.

Elsewhere we are using ivies to cover the soil, walls and even trees. Most of those we use began life with us as house plants. There is Glacier ivy, grey and green variegated, planted around the base of the old pear where we have built a low wall and used the ivy foliage to fill the circular space around the base of the trunk. A variety which had its leaves feathered with white and sometimes rose has been encouraged to climb on the north side of the wall by the gate and has reached and is beginning to clothe the top of the wall. The pretty Gold Heart ivy, with bright yellow zones to its leaf centres, has been planted to cover the ground below a wide-spreading potentilla at the edge of the garden. This should clothe the break between the gravel of the drive and the soil of the border and it will also provide winter colour when the shrub is bare. Another of the same variety has been planted at the base of the apple tree which in its branches bears the wild *Clematis vitalba*. Here the main colour theme of the border is

yellow and the ivy should be useful in winter. The tree is so obviously on its last legs that it might as well now serve a decorative purpose, having been utilitarian at some earlier point. Elsewhere we have a low bank clothed with spreading cotoneasters and here a Glacier ivy again covers the soil below the branches. Tiny variegated leaves of Little Diamond ivy are gradually covering the edges of the paving stones in another area. More will be used if and when the occasion presents itself.

Since we have taken over a little extra piece of land at the bottom of our garden we have begun thinking seriously about a wild garden. Some shrubs and little trees are there already but I want to plant certain herbaceous and other plants that will not only need little attention but which will also look at home. So that I can see it from the other end of the plot I may plant a stand of the giant cow parsnip, *Heracleum villosum*, sometimes called the cartwheel flower because of its size.

At the other end of the scale I intend to plant tiny hardy cyclamen, fritillaries and other little bulb flowers, primroses and other primulas, hostas, ferns and climbers such as honeysuckles, clematises, and polygonum for the trees.

Hedera helix Gold Heart, a striking variegated ivy. It has a neat habit of growth and makes a handsome screening plant with its rich cream and green leaves, which are especially welcome in winter

Flowers for Special Places

Every garden, however pretty, has its eyesores and areas that present problems to gardeners – and some are not always what one would expect! Judging by the letters I receive from readers the metal man-hole cover seems to be a problem in some gardens. A little sink garden makes as good a cover as any if you are certain that there will be someone nearby who could move it should the man-hole cover ever have to be opened for inspection. Near my own covers I am planting a selection of plants that will sprawl and screen them – *Cotoneaster horizontalis*, *Senecio greyii*, and santolina among them. These can be held back temporarily by bamboo canes if the covers have to be removed.

One other way to hide a man-hole cover is to stand a group of plants in containers over it. A piece of neatly fitting asbestos or a thin paving stone would camouflage it nicely and serve as a base for the tubs.

Dustbins, coal bunkers and sheds are also a problem. Most of these can be camouflaged by climbers trained over the greater part of them or round them to block out the view of the eyesore from a window or from a favourite sitting-out place in the garden. Plastic-covered meshes such as Netlon are a great help here because not only can they be easily fastened to a wall but they can be curved and bent easily. Even if you cannot manage to install a strong support round which to curve the mesh, you will find that stout bamboos threaded vertically through the mesh and hammered into the soil are very efficient. Once you have made an attractive and efficient screen you will find that there are plenty of not too heavy climbers which can be grown against them. One I use is *Eccremocarpus scaber*, an awful name for a pretty little orange-flowered perennial climber so easily raised from seed. Honeysuckles, including the attractive evergreen, variegated *Lonicera japonica aureo reticulata*, and clematis can weave among each other.

The fast-growing Russian vine, *Polygonum baldschuanicum*, which becomes smothered with a white foam of flowers in late summer, should only be used if you have plenty of space and a strong support. The early-flowering *Clematis montana* is better and this is also almost evergreen. I grow this combined with the almost evergreen rambler rose Albéric Barbier.

An ugly drainpipe can be covered with lengths of Netlon and used to support an attractive climber. Since the business side of plumbing is on the back of the house, most often the north side, you should choose the climbers carefully. You want hardy honeysuckles and winter jasmine, or, if you can give it a fairly sheltered angle in the wall, the pretty *Clematis calycina* which has unusual fern-like leaves and bears creamy-white flowers early in the year.

On the south walls the other clematises, summer jasmine (*Jasminum officinale*), *Campsis radicans*, with vivid trumpet-like flowers in September, the passion flower (*Passiflora caerulea*) or even wisteria may be grown in this way.

If you do not want to grow a permanent climber there are many lovely annuals or perennials which, because they are tender, are treated as annuals, and may be grown instead. Among these are the familiar sweet peas, particularly Galaxy; climbing nasturtium, its cousin the yellow canary creeper and the vivid flame flower, *Tropaeolum speciosum*; *Cobaea scandens* or the cup-and-saucer flower; ipomoea or morning glory; thunbergia or Black-eyed Susan, and the ornamental hop, *Humulus japonicus variegatus*. You can also grow the more attractive of the edible runner beans, Blue Coco, for example; and marrows and squashes.

Old trees also need to be dressed up in some way. For those above 6 ft., climbing roses and ramblers are suitable and these may be grown in harmony with clematis. For a tree (or a wall) facing north, try the fragrant rose Madame Alfred Carrière, with lovely blushing double white flowers. Others are Madame Grégoire Staechelin, an old-fashioned deep pink variety, and the lovely, floriferous Albertine. All will grow if you prepare a good root area for them. Plant them so that the prevailing wind blows them into and not away from the tree.

As well as clematis in trees, as I described in the previous chapter, another very pretty sight I once saw in autumn was of a tree draped with white *Polygonum baldschuanicum* mingling with the scarlet leaves of Virginian creeper.

Tall tree stumps can have rose shoots trained round spiral-wise (roses bloom best when the stems are trained horizontally as far as possible). The climbing *Hydrangea petiolaris*, eccremocarpus, and jasmines will all climb trees. In fact you can try almost any climber you like. The most important things are to give it some good soil and watch that it doesn't become dry in its early stages and to coax it to climb in the beginning.

Tree stumps are best hidden so that one can forget all about them! Annuals such as nasturtiums

Hydrangea petiolaris, a magnificent self-clinging climber, will grow to a considerable height when trained up a tree. It flowers in summer

are quick and effective but not lasting. A *Cotoneaster horizontalis* will embrace the stump and quite quickly hide it. With this sprawling plant you could plant a group of *Helleborus lividus* as a contrast to the dark green. You could also pin a flowering quince over the trunk and let it grow slowly to a dense bush. A cover is quickly made by slicing off a root of stonecrop, pushing a spade under it and carrying it to the stump. Place it on the top and leave the rest to nature.

From trees to the shade they cast. Most plants that enjoy shade like their conditions to be moist and the soil rich but the plants grown in the shade of trees and sometimes of buildings, too, are affected by the amount of drip to which they are subjected and will die if it is too great. If you have a small garden and are short of space, remember that in their natural surroundings most wild plants, herbaceous, bulbous and shrubby alike, will, if all the other conditions are right, grow quite close to the trunks of many trees.

If you are going to plant under a tree, a large tree, I think that it is better to build up a bed of soil for the plants rather than to try and dig holes. Make the bed of good soil. You can use your garden soil provided you mix in plenty of good humus material with it.

Keep herbaceous plants well watered until they become established.

Most plants that grow naturally in the shade of trees grow also in the decomposing leaves and debris rained down by the tree itself. They like both the food and the cool texture of such rich humus, so allow the leaves to remain. Not many plants are happy under conifers; the regular dropping of the needles makes the soil toxic to other plants. To avoid this these should be raked and taken away regularly and the soil both limed and manured, though not at the time time. As a tonic, feed the soil under trees with bonemeal, hoof and horn meal, compost, animal and seaweed manures, in fact, any organic fertilizer.

Many flowering shrubs grow well in the shade and for herbaceous perennials that like shade there is a list of suitable plants for such conditions on page 50.

In other places where there is shade for only part of the day there are many shrubs one can grow.

Where the soil is peaty or non-limy, andromeda, gaultheria, cornus, azaleas and rhododendrons will do quite well. On ordinary soil, *Berberis aquifolium* and *B. darwinii*, escallonia, *Rosa eglanteria*, the sweet eglantine, *Rosa rugosa* and *Spiraea douglasii* are just a few that will give you attractive foliage and blossom.

You can grow some herbaceous plants with these shrubs or at the edge of a planting of trees. The tall late-summer flowering *Anemone japonica*, the spring-flowering yellow daisy doronicum or leopard's bane (which will grow wild in the grass, too, along with aquilegia or columbine), dicentra (bleeding heart), digitalis (foxglove), hellebore (the Christmas and Lenten rose family), lily of the valley, *Saxifraga umbrosa* (London pride) and both oenothera (the evening primrose) and the true primrose will grow splendidly in these conditions and give you flowers for cutting, too.

If there is a good spell of sunshine or daylight each day, say three or four hours, then many of the so-called lilies will bloom well and give distinction to your garden. The hemerocallis or day lilies are a good example, and the new varieties of these are

A good plant to choose for a partially shaded position is *Oenothera biennis*, the fragrant yellow evening primrose

really wonderful. Hosta or plantain lilies, sometimes listed as funkia, have extremely lovely leaves, some variegated, some grey-green and glaucous, and all of them ideal for flower arrangement since they are so long lasting and show off their large individual 'lilies' of delicate lavender so beautifully.

Among the annuals which you can grow in shade are ageratum; the canary creeper, which you can allow to scramble as well as climb; impatiens; African and French marigolds; mimulus and nicotiana. Begonias are also suitable for such conditions.

If you have an oak tree, or more than one, consider yourself fortunate for the oak is a fine mother tree whose roots go down so deep that they do not rob the plants beneath the branches. The dappled shade cast by oaks is ideal for all the rhododendron family.

And don't forget that if summer- and autumn-flowering plants present too much of a problem you are almost certain to be able to grow the spring- and autumn-flowering bulbs.

Flowers for Winter

Most winter flowers really begin to open a little in October and November. After that, everything depends upon the weather. In prolonged snow and frost no plant can be expected to produce and keep its frail flowers fresh and lovely. But many will open on normal cold days and some low-growing shrubs, such as heathers, will go on blooming even under the snow.

A great deal depends on locality, of course; the mild south-west and other areas affected by the Gulf Stream are bound to be kinder to the plants. Quite a lot also depends on what shelter the plants have. Warm spots among and under trees, if you have them, are places where frost will not damage plants as severely as it might elsewhere. A warm wall, or a corner made by walls at right angles to each other will protect and even mildly force certain plants into early bloom.

There are some winter-flowering plants which do well on the north side of the house, perhaps because there are no great extremes of cold and sunshine. Camellias, for example, have glossier leaves when given this aspect and winter jasmine will clothe a north wall with its yellow stars.

The sight of a camellia bush covered in blooms shining in the winter sun and contrasting gloriously against the dark green gleaming leaves is such a wonderful sight that I am surprised no more are grown. Yet except for a little care in the early stages, when the soil over the roots should be well mulched with peat to protect them from frost, they are no trouble at all. They grow slowly and neatly and flower from an early age. Camellias once established and growing well are so floriferous that when frost damages the blooms they produce others in a very short time. They are, in fact, hardier than most people realize. In January *Camellia japonica nobilissima* will begin flowering and go on until March. *C. williamsii*, a cross between *C. japonica* and *C. saluenensis* and with single and semi-double varieties, is known as the perpetual-flowering camellia, blooming as it does from January to April. There are other kinds, some of which need a really sheltered garden or the protection of a cold greenhouse.

Camellias grow well in a neutral soil (they can always be mulched with peat) but not in an alkaline soil. They prefer an acid soil. The ideal pH is about $5 \cdot 0$, though they will tolerate a higher pH than rhododendrons. They will also flourish in heavy soils. The best fertilizer for them is bonemeal, this being applied annually with peat as a top dressing, in a proportion of 14 lb. of bonemeal to 1 cwt. of peat.

The winter-flowering ericas are pretty, useful plants. Not only do they provide colour through so many months of the year, but during the rest of the time they furnish the garden attractively, covering the soil with a nice mat of green and keeping down weeds. These also are plants you can grow quite close to the lawn; should you mow them as you get to the edge they will be none the worse for it. I like also to use them to clothe those areas of soil which adjoin gravel paths as they prevent the soil from washing down into the gravel and make an attractive link between one and the other.

One more thing in their favour is that they have blooms of various hues. The plants change colour as the flower buds begin to form and this colour intensifies as the plant draws near its flowering time. When the flowers fade they are a pleasant russet and so provide more colour. The plants can be clipped in May to keep them short and neat.

Erica carnea and its varieties will tolerate a little lime but the emphasis must be on the *little*. Chalk is too limy. *E. darleyensis* is a hybrid I warmly recommend. It will grow to nearly 2 ft. tall and flowers from November to April.

Larger heathers include *E. arborea alpina,* the tree heath, which grows to 8 ft. and *E. mediterranea,* from 4 to 10 ft. tall. There are also shorter varieties of *mediterranea.* The flowers of *arborea* appear in early March, and are followed by those of *mediterranea,* which continue to May.

Not very flamboyant but with a graceful charm of its own is another member of the erica family, the evergreen *Leucothoë catesbaei,* which will grow as high as 6 ft. The slender, arching branches, on which the small white flowers are borne in long rows of short racemes, are graceful for winter decoration. There are also *L. davisiae,* also evergreen, and *L. racemosa,* a deciduous species. They enjoy a light peaty soil and dislike lime.

Viburnums are shrubs for all gardens. Many flower through the winter and are very fragrant; a branch or two in the house will scent a whole room. Possibly the best known, though, is one which is not so fragrant − *Viburnum tinus,* commonly known as laurustinus. *V. carlesii,* a most sweetly scented plant, is supposed to flower in April but in a sheltered place you will find it in bloom earlier. *V.* Park Farm Hybrid flowers earlier but is not so scented.

The delicately scented yellow flowers of *Jasminum nudiflorum,* the winter jasmine, are a pretty sight on dark winter days

V. macrocephalum is not very hardy and should be grown only in sheltered gardens or in a cold greenhouse. It has green flowers, which change to pure white in March. The hybrid *V. bodnantense* Dawn flowers for Christmas.

There are several early-flowering clematis, though most are spring-flowering plants. However, if you can give it protection from frost, *C. calycina* will produce creamy-white, freckled flowers in January and February.

I think that the plant my family loves most is our *Prunus subhirtella autumnalis,* the winter-flowering cherry, with small delicately pink flower petals the colour of a wild rose. Ours begins to flower in late October and goes on through the winter. In a recent mild winter it was in full blossom for months and even in late May when it was in full leaf it was still possible to find some flowers.

Cherries or prunus are the first trees to bloom and there are a surprising number of varieties of *Prunus subhirtella. P. pseudocerasus* (syn. *P. cantabrigiensis*) is one of the earliest if it is given a sheltered spot. All are good trees for the small garden and cherries are accommodating plants which do well both on chalk and on soil suitable for rhododendrons! But the area for the tree must be well prepared and enriched because too much lime can cause chlorosis, a yellowing of the leaves and other deficiencies. They must have very good drainage or they will suffer from winter wet rot which can kill the trees.

63

Among the rhododendrons are some of the best of the winter-flowering shrubs, in sufficient variety to suit everyone's taste. Just remember that the more hairs there are on a rhododendron's leaves, the less hardy it is, so buy the glossy-leaved types. *Rhododendron* Christmas Cheer really does flower at Christmas. Pick it when the buds are showing colour and remove some of the leaves. *R. mucronulatum* flowers in January. *R. praecox* flowers from early February to March. There are others, so consult your nurseryman for details.

The lovely Christmas rose, *Helleborus niger*, will flower for Christmas if you give it a little encouragement. Plant in October, November or March but don't expect much for the first year. See that the soil is rich or enriched before planting and that it is deep and full of humus. In the wild, hellebores are found growing in the leafy soil of woods.

In April help the plant to begin preparing for winter. Liberally mulch the ground with well-rotted manure or garden compost. Failing this, use Plus fertilizer and leafmould. During a dry summer water the plants freely. I like to use a deep mulch of lawn mowings to keep the soil moist and to prevent me, or anyone else, from disturbing the roots.

When you see the flower buds, if you want to gather the blooms, cover the plant with a cloche which will both protect them and force them gently. To keep the blooms immaculate in the border, cover the soil surface with moss and place a few slug pellets under it as a precaution.

There are several hellebores, all of them handsome plants. They are perfect to grow among shrubs or in a wild garden, if you are lucky enough to have one. Divide the roots in March. Sow seed in a cold frame in October or March.

If you can find a patch of poor limy soil be sure to plant the Algerian iris, *Iris unguicularis*, formerly and still sometimes called *I. stylosa*. It is important to tuck it away out of sight for it is neither a pretty nor a tidy plant, but the flowers are its feature. Lavender hued and sweet scented, they are hidden down in the grass-like leaves and you have to search for them. Gather them in bud. Give the Algerian iris a south-facing situation. Plant or divide it in March and watch for and prevent slugs. During the summer, tidy the plant by pulling away the dead and dried leaves.

Once the shortest day has passed you can expect to see some movement in the trees and shrubs, the bulbs peeping above the ground and the

Chimonanthus praecox, the winter sweet. The fragrant yellow flowers appear in January and February

primroses opening. Somehow, the pussy willow seems to appear suddenly, yet if you look closely you will find the furry catkins lying flat against the stem as soon as winter starts. Cut a few branches and they will open indoors. *Salix discolor* is the wild pussy willow. *S. daphnoides*, the violet willow, has catkins which are violet tinted.

The grey-green catkins of *Garrya elliptica*, a plant for a south or west wall or a sheltered shrub border, are extremely graceful and look lovely with stems of viburnum blossom.

When I was a little girl I loved to walk along by Old Widcombe Church in Bath on a winter's day because there, near the churchyard wall, was a fine arbutus or strawberry tree. I think that the white, wax-like flowers fascinated me as much as the pendant strawberry-like fruits. This really is a beautiful tree with lovely deep evergreen foliage. It belongs to the heather family and the flowers are like great heather bells. Although this family prefers sandy peat, *Arbutus unedo* will grow on chalk.

There are a surprising number of shrubs which blossom during the shortest days and it seems to me that I walk more often round my garden, cutting a little here, a little there, during this time than at any other. I think it must be because we all want to be reassured that spring is coming.

From just before Christmas I can start cutting a selection from them, mostly when they are still in bud so that they can open out slowly indoors. This way we can have a succession of winter posies. There are usually a few primroses, snowdrops, iris, early crocuses, and daisies to nestle at the foot of stems of the shrubs in these arrangements. The purple-studded stems of daphne are always very sweet.

Cornus mas comes very early and seems to go on and on until in early spring the bush is hazy yellow. A few individual stems from the clusters at the stem ends of *Mahonia bealei* bring the scent of lily of the valley and somehow, although they open some flowers in winter, the periwinkles seem to bring a touch of summer.

Many of the bulbs, corms and tubers begin to bloom early in the year and I have given full descriptions of these in Chapters 1 and 2, 'Flowers from Bulbs and Corms' and 'Flowers from Tubers'. You will also find more about winter flowers in Chapter 4 'Flowers from Shrubs and Trees'.

You can expect the following plants to be in bloom throughout the winter, but sometimes you may have the extra bonus of border flowers, primroses, marigolds, bergenia, arabis, daisies and flowering currant – it all depends on the weather.

NOVEMBER. *Arbutus unedo, Erica carnea, Garrya elliptica, Jasminum nudiflorum, Mahonia japonica, M. bealei, Prunus subhirtella autumnalis, Viburnum bodnantense, V. fragrans, V. tinus* and vinca (periwinkle).

DECEMBER. As above, also *Galanthus byzantinus* (snowdrop), *Helleborus niger* and *Iris unguicularis*.

JANUARY. As above and also *Anemone blanda, Clematis calycina, Eranthis hyemalis, Salix discolor* and *S. daphnoides*.

FEBRUARY. As above, also, *Bulbocodium vernum* (spring meadow saffron), *Chimonanthus praecox, Cornus mas, Corylopsis spicata,* crocus species, *Iris reticulata, Narcissus* February Gold and others, and *Stachyurus praecox*.

The graceful grey-green catkins of *Garrya elliptica* are a welcome addition to the winter scene. The male form produces the finest catkins

Bottom: A colourful bed of roses and mixed bedding plants. At the back of the border runner beans have been trained to form a screen, an interesting way of treating a plant which is both useful and decorative

Opposite: Hemerocallis, the day lilies, seen on the right, will flower well in a partially shaded position with some sun each day. Also shown are lupins, delphiniums, astilbes and *Chrysanthemum* Esther Read

Flowers for Pots and Containers

On my travels round the country I see literally hundreds of gardens every year and I am always struck by the thought that they could be so much more colourful and effective if only the house and garden were not so sharply divided. I believe that the house should extend or spill over into the garden and that the plants in the garden, or some of them at least, should peep into the house. If you do this, particularly with a small garden, you will be surprised to discover just how many more plants you can grow and how easy it is to extend both the productive and the decorative areas of the garden.

If you have no greenhouse to provide you with flowers out of season, remember that even a covered porch or balcony affords protection for those subjects which need it in winter. And if you have no garden to speak of you can grow a fantastic number of plants in containers. One of the brightest sights I ever saw was in Exmouth, where a terrace house without a garden was smothered in flowers which appeared to be planted in every kind of container, hanging from doors, windows and walls!

But it is vital to remember that this is an artificial form of gardening and your plants will not be happy, and won't look well, unless you have provided the essentials. The container itself is less important than the way it is filled. Roots, like everything else, will die without air, so finding a way to aerate the soil is most important.

To do this you need to line the base of any kind of container with what is known as a drainage layer. Traditionally this is of crocks (pieces of broken flower pot), but not everyone has these, so broken china, washed clinker or pebbles can be used. You can also use small stones, shingle for example, but stones are heavy and may make it impossible for you to move the containers. On the other hand they anchor them well if this is what is needed.

I sometimes use charcoal in my containers. It is quite cheap, very light and can be used again and again with the added advantage that it keeps the soil sweet. It is possible also to drop a few charcoal pellets over crocks and stones.

The more drainage you have the healthier will the soil be but you should not use so much material that there is no room left for the soil and the plants! The minimum drainage depth should be an inch. The deeper the container the deeper the drainage layer should be.

Soil is important and it can also be expensive.

Ideally you need a well-balanced mixture like one of the John Innes potting composts which you can buy from garden shops and centres. These are based on sterilized soils which means that weeds, disease spores and all insects present in the soil are killed and you get off to a good start.

If you want to mix your own soil you will need 7 parts good garden loam, 3 parts peat and/or leafmould, and 2 parts sand. To this you should add 2 parts by weight of hoof and horn meal, 2 parts superphosphate of lime and 1 part sulphate of potash. This is added to the mixture at the rate of 4 oz. to a bushel and with it goes $\frac{3}{4}$ oz. of ground chalk. All these ingredients can be bought from garden shops. Incidentally, if you have a garden and plenty of soil, you would find it worth while to invest in a soil sterilizer. Mine is electrically heated, takes a bushel of soil at a time and I find it is very useful.

Since soil is heavy, those of you with roof gardens, balconies or window boxes might be interested in something much lighter. There are now several soilless, peat-based composts on the market which are extremely light in weight until they are watered. Some are all purpose and some are prepared for seed sowing or for potting. I find them useful and easy to handle, but I do not think they replace soil composts entirely. Unlike soils, it is almost impossible to overwater these peat-based composts, but on the other hand if they are allowed to become too dry it takes a little patience to get them to absorb water again.

Although both kinds of potting mixtures contain plant foods you should remember that because you have to water plants in containers so liberally the essential minerals are being constantly washed out. This means that once your plants are growing well they should be fed regularly as well as watered. Water first, and then give a soluble plant food; there are plenty of good ones on the market. I really cannot stress too much that all outdoor plants in containers need a lot of water in dry weather. I so often see hanging baskets, originally well filled but no longer at all attractive because

A pavement garden outside a town house. A wide variety of plants can be grown in containers such as window boxes and tubs to provide colour all summer in an urban setting

Bottom: The lovely Christmas rose, *Helleborus niger*, really does flower at Christmas if given a little encouragement. It requires a rich soil with plenty of humus

Opposite top: Verbenas beneath a wall screened by over-hanging cotoneasters. The sprawling *Cotoneaster horizontalis* and *C. microphyllus* are useful screening plants and their cheerful red berries are particularly welcome in winter

Opposite bottom: Of all the winter-flowering shrubs perhaps none is more beautiful than the exotic camellia, with its dark, shining leaves and waxy blooms. This is a *Camellia williamsii* hybrid

the plants are dying of drought. If you have a hanging basket make certain either that it can be lowered easily for watering or that you have a pair of safe steps for reaching it.

When you fill your window boxes or any other type of container make sure that the soil does not come right up to the rim; leave at least an inch so that when the container is watered you have room for the water and you do not wash the soil out. It is good for the plant's roots if the water rushes through the soil when it is first poured in, as it will drag air down with it. But you must realize that the soil will not be wet enough at this stage, so give more water.

There are many kinds of attractive, suitable containers for plants. The first thing to ensure is that the container is deep enough. It should be possible to stand a pot 5 in. in diameter inside it so that its rim comes just below the level of the container. If it is not as deep as this there will not be room enough for any plants taken from this size pot, and shallow containers dry out too rapidly.

The range of plants you can grow in this way is very wide. In summer, bedding plants, which are annuals or half-hardy annuals, make a gay show. These are usually sold as good-sized plants and are not long in coming into bloom. Most of them will adapt themselves to being grown in a container rather than the ground.

I often find container gardens are very gaudy, with red pelargoniums (pot geraniums), deep blue lobelia and yellow calceolarias, but there are enough varieties and types of other plants to have a more subtle colour harmony. Think about having a colour scheme which ties in with your curtains, or the paint on your house or the coloured paving round it. Think also of the advantages of all white, or all yellow schemes. Flowers in these colours shine prettily through the twilight, so if you are sitting out of doors you can enjoy them until the last moment.

A contrast of shapes and habits in the plants makes a container garden more interesting. You want some which will grow upright, some which will spread and others which will cascade. Plant from the centre outwards or, if the container is against a wall, from the back to the front. When you plant trailers see that they are tilted a little, and already set to go the way you want them.

Among the hardy annuals, sweet-scented alyssum shows up well in town but if you have whitewashed walls you might like to grow a coloured variety

instead. This plant will trail attractively over the edge. Other annual trailers are lobelia (the light blues are very lovely), verbena, petunias, mesembryanthemum, phacelia and nemophila. Trailing begonias are also very attractive.

Some can be raised from seed sown directly into the containers, but the trouble with this is that you will have quite a long period with an empty-looking container, although if you have grown spring bulbs you can sow annual seeds above them.

Hardy annuals can be sown in September and allowed to grow through the winter. But the trouble with these, pretty though they are, is that they do not have such a long flowering season as the half-hardy kinds. Although you cannot plant the latter until all fear of the young plants being killed by frost has passed, at least they go on flowering until the first frosts arrive.

One compromise solution is almost to fill your container with half-hardy plants which you have either grown from seed or bought, and then to sow

A fine specimen of *Lilium regale*, the regal lily, grown in a large container. Many summer-flowering plants with bulbous or fleshy roots make excellent container plants

a little seed among them. Nasturtium seeds, for example, are large enough to be pressed individually into the soil.

These flowers, and the canary creeper, are very showy but the black aphid is always attracted to them so you will have to spray the plants. I recommend regular spraying with a systemic insecticide like Abol X. This type of insecticide will only kill insects which are sucking the plant tissues, although it *will* kill others if they become wetted during spraying. So wait until late in the day, when the bees and others stop visiting the flowers before you spray and do not spray if you see ladybirds on the plants because they eat aphids. Prevention is best. Spray early in the season and after that at regular intervals as directed.

As children we sang about 'wallflowers growing up so high' and there can be few of us who haven't seen snapdragons (antirrhinums) blooming along the top of an old wall, and yet these two pretty sweet-scented plants are often overlooked by the balcony or window box gardener. Wallflowers are for a spring show but the snapdragons will go on and on if you take care to remove the faded flowers and don't allow the seed to form.

The Bijou and other dwarf forms of sweet peas will also do well in containers and flower over a long period. Petunias are wonderful in good weather. Unfortunately the Grandiflora F_1 hybrids are not rain resistant and become pulp-like and horrible during long wet spells. Some of the Multiflora hybrids, on the other hand, are much better, though wet days are not really for petunias. F_1 Resisto mixed colours and the lovely white Polar Cap are good varieties.

You may prefer to grow something more permanent in your containers. In this case you will find that some shrubs are quite happy in tubs. The camellia is the perfect tub plant. Rhododendrons, azaleas, pieris and kalmia are also good flowering evergreens – all needing peaty soil. If you live in a limy district you should use rain water for them. Keep them out of strong winds and remember to give all these plants partial shade, so that they are not baked at the hottest part of the day. If you can't do this it is better to grow something else.

If the tub is really large enough you can grow a greater variety of shrubs and even small trees. I have seen *Prunus triloba*, the double peach (also fruiting peaches), malus (ornamental crab apples), laburnum, roses, wisteria, *Polygonum baldschuanicum*, oranges and lemons grown in this way.

Fuchsias are ideally suited for tubs, boxes and hanging baskets, where the pendant varieties will hang down so very prettily. But you must never forget to water or feed them! You can have standard fuchsias as well as bushes. You can also buy standard marguerites, heliotrope and pelargoniums.

Some perennials can be treated as temporary plants. Doronicum, the pretty yellow spring daisy, planted in autumn above tulip bulbs which are positioned well under the soil surface, will bloom at the same time. I once saw black tulips with yellow doronicums grown in this way.

So many bulbs can be grown in tubs, from the familiar spring-flowering kinds to gladioli, acidanthera, tigridia and lilies. Other plants with rhizomes or thick fleshy root stocks, such as the blue agapanthus (African lily), make fine tub plants. These will need to be given protection during winter. The tubs are best placed under the staging in a greenhouse and kept dry. Alternatively, they could go in a frost-proof shed. Be sure to water the plants freely in dry weather in summer.

Hydrangeas are popular container plants but the poor plants so often suffer by being displayed in full sun where they wilt very quickly simply because they cannot take up enough water to keep them turgid under such conditions. Remember, they enjoy cool shade.

Other plants for shade include begonias, impatiens (Busy Lizzie), pansies, Creeping Jenny, London pride, heliotrope, gloxinias, polyanthus and bulbous flowers.

Possibly the most popular container plants are the cheerful pelargoniums, usually called geraniums, although the latter are really hardy herbaceous border plants, otherwise called crane's bills. Pelargoniums are divided into several groups which are quite easy to recognize. Those with a dark or contrasting zone or mark on their leaves (sometimes it may only be a faint band of darker green) are called zonal pelargoniums. They have flowers of other hues besides pillar-box red! Those which we like to use in hanging baskets, at the edge of troughs or window boxes, or even to climb a wall, which they will do if they are given support, are known as ivy-leaved pelargoniums.

The tricolour varieties, which have three distinct colours in their leaves in beautiful harmonies, do not usually have fine blooms but some are more conspicuous than others. Bicolours have green and white leaves.

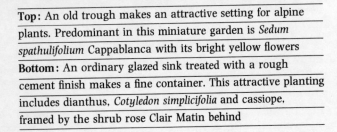

Top: An old trough makes an attractive setting for alpine plants. Predominant in this miniature garden is *Sedum spathulifolium* Cappablanca with its bright yellow flowers
Bottom: An ordinary glazed sink treated with a rough cement finish makes a fine container. This attractive planting includes dianthus, *Cotyledon simplicifolia* and cassiope, framed by the shrub rose Clair Matin behind

Centre: Full use has been made here of balcony, urns and hanging baskets to grow fuchsias, pelargoniums, petunias and even roses
Right: Container planting helps to bridge the gap between garden and home. In this delightful pavement garden fuchsia, lobelia, alyssum and petunias have been planted at different levels to make the most of a small area

Miniature Flowers and Sink Gardens

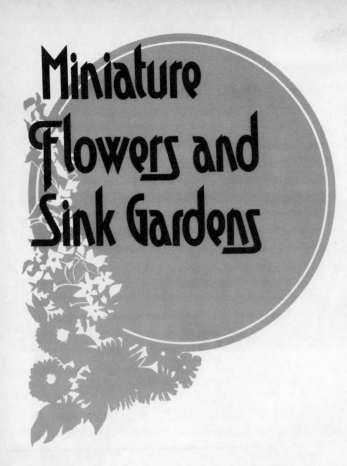

Miniature flowers have an irresistible appeal. There is something about them which is touching and somehow wonderful. Whereas in large gardens they tend to look lost unless they are grown in great masses, if you have only a small garden, or no garden at all, you can grow really tiny plants such as alpines on a scale which suits them.

One of the favourite containers for a miniature garden is an old stone sink, but stone sinks are not now quite so easy to come by. Some garden suppliers specialize in plant sinks or troughs made from modern materials, many of them mounted on a stone plinth which can look pleasant enough.

In fact, you can see some very attractive little examples near the alpine house at The Royal Horticultural Society gardens at Wisley, Surrey.

Plain white glazed sinks are more easily obtained, but they tend to look harsh and need a little treatment before they blend harmoniously with both the plants or the surroundings. The best way to do this is to paint the surface with Polybond, then, when it's dry, paint it with a mixture of cement, sand and peat, in roughly equal quantities, made soft enough to apply with the hand.

Leave the drainage hole unplugged. Cover the bottom of the sink with a layer of broken flower pots, crushed brick, or small pieces of charcoal. Over this, spread a 1-in.-deep layer of coarse peat or leafmould. You can use ready-mixed John Innes potting soil, with the addition of extra grit or coarse sand to make the soil nice and open and well drained. The ingredients must be well mixed and moistened but not sodden. Half fill the sink. Landscape it with rocks, making little plateaux for some plants and snug places for others. Since alpines are always sold in pots you can experiment as you work, placing a plant here, another there until you have the setting you want. You can then turn the plants out of their containers and surround the root balls with soil. Make sure that the plants are well firmed in position, top up with soil, leaving a space of 1 or 2 in. between soil and sink rim. When you have finished planting, cover the soil surface with granite or limestone chippings. These will prevent the soil from drifting away and they will also keep the little plants cool.

There are other suitable containers you might be able to find, like large earthenware cream-crocks. I once saw a delightful little garden in an old blue and white wash basin and my neighbour has made a pretty one in a pig's long feeding trough — of all things!

The essential things are that the container should be wide and at least 3 in. deep. This will allow 1 in. at the bottom for drainage materials such as broken flower pots, crushed brick, shingle or charcoal or a mixture of all of these.

There is a surprising number of small plants suitable for this type of garden. You can buy many of them at garden centres and all from an alpine plant specialist. With your flowers you may like to have some little evergreen trees and shrubs. All the following are attractive in bloom:

Androsace carnea and varieties, *A. sempervivoides*
Arenaria
Armeria caespitosa, *A.c. alba*, *A. caespitosa* Bevan's Variety
Asperula lilaciflora caespitosa, *A. nitida*, *A. suberosa*
Campanula arvatica, *C. a. alba*, *C. pulla*
Dianthus freynii, *D. microlepis*, *D. myrtinervis*, *D. subacaulis*
Douglasia laevigata, *D. montana*
Draba bryoides imbricata, *D. dedeana*, *D. rigida*
Erinus alpinus
Erodium chamaedryoides (heron's bill), *E.c. roseum*, *E. corsicum*
Gentiana verna and *G. verna angulosa*. A friend of mine grows these well. All through the summer months she pours the still cold but thawed water from the de-frosted refrigerator over the soil round the roots of this plant to simulate the cool mountain streams they are used to.

Geranium farreri
Globularia cordifolia (blue daisy), *G. nana*, *G. stygia*
Iris lacustris, *I. rubro-marginata*
Petrocallis pyrenaica
Polygala calcarea (milkwort)
Raoulia australis, *R. glabra*, *R. lutescens*
Saxifraga, cushion types
Silene acaulis (catchfly), *S.a. alba*
Viola blanda, *V. gracilis* (syn. *V. olympica*), *V. saxatilis aetolica*.

There are a few charming little flowering shrubs but these are not really suitable for any but the large sink garden. In my own I have a tiny broom, *Genista pulchella*, only 3 in. high, and a tiny berberis. You can also have helianthemums, jasmines,

A trough fashioned from natural stone makes the best looking container garden, but these are becoming very hard to obtain

Left: Scented plants can be found among those growing at the waterside as well as in the border, such as the pretty *Primula florindae*, shown here in the foreground

Top: The old-fashioned favourite mignonette (*Reseda odorata*) is well worth growing for its glorious scent. It is sometimes hard to establish, preferring a soil liberally scattered with lime

Bottom: *Nicotiana affinis*, the tobacco flower, is deliciously scented, especially noticeable on warm summer evenings

polygala, rhododendron, salix (willow), spiraea and veronica as well as miniature roses.

I once saw a number of these little shrubs and other miniature plants growing between the stones in a tiny paved garden which was a charming and sensible way to display them. You can also grow them in a raised bed made on a stone wall.

Some years ago in Constance Wheatcroft's garden, where you would expect to see fabulous roses, I was enchanted with a border of miniature roses made round a pond. It was thick with bloom and very pretty.

True miniature roses really deserve the name by which the Victorians knew them – fairy roses. The neatest and smallest of them all is *Rosa roulettii*, which is said to have been rediscovered growing in a little village in Switzerland after miniatures had fallen from favour. More than that, this rose was said to have been growing in the same pot for over a century! This would seem to indicate that roses may be pot grown and that they certainly should grow in a sink garden, but, generally speaking, rose growers do not recommend this because a sink has not enough depth and all roses like a deep root run.

The charming little *R. roulettii* is a parent of many other dwarf or miniature roses, Cinderella, blush pink and double, being one of them. Others include Pour Toi, a charming, perfectly formed cream rose, and Rosina or Josephine Wheatcroft, which is a beautiful yellow, prettily shaped and with a lovely foliage.

Some miniatures grow much taller than others and are more strictly dwarf roses than fairy types. Baby Masquerade is one of the dwarf ones I have growing among my lilies. It is bushy, about 1 ft. high and very gay when it is in bloom with semi-double yellow and pink flowers. Humpty Dumpty reminds me of the old-fashioned rambler rose flowers, for it is really double. The plant is short and neat. There are only a few of these roses, but more are coming along each year, so do study the rosegrowers' catalogues.

The so-called fairy roses, which you can grow very easily from seed, are usually single and almost white although there may be a few which are pink. They are not flamboyant but very sweet like tiny wild roses and make a pretty low hedge – they look particularly attractive in a double hedge with lavender.

If ever you get the chance to go to a spring flower show don't miss it, for there may be an opportunity to see many exquisite miniature narcissi. A few bulb growers specialize in them. Although some, like the hoop-petticoat daffodil, colour banks and the meadow at Wisley and other great gardens, growing almost wild, most miniatures are best grown in little plateaux on a rock garden so that you know where they are! They must also be protected from slugs where these are a nuisance. You will see from the chapter on bulbs that there are many other wild flowers which can be grown in this way.

There are also miniature tulips, fritillarias and other plants, some of them rare, but those are best grown in an alpine house.

If you have a rock garden this enables you to grow many charming small flowers. As I write, little pictures of them spring immediately to mind – tiny azaleas, cushiony and mossy saxifragas studded with blooms; incredibly tiny gypsophilas, hypericum, helianthemum, linaria; heaths, like little cushions studded with jewelled pins; roses, Dresden china daisies, baby campanulas, nail-sized dianthus, foot-high *Fuchsia pumila*, lilliput willows, crane's bills, phloxes and the unbelievably beautiful

Fritillaria meleagris, a delightful miniature fritillary, is known as the snake's head fritillary

rhodohypoxis. In fact, a visit to an alpine specialist's nursery is well worth while.

An alpine house can bring a great deal of pleasure, especially to those who no longer enjoy working in the open during the winter months. This means a greenhouse designed to imitate the light, airy, low-humidity conditions found in the mountains. At the same time it offers protection from storm damage and from sudden variations of weather. It is always well ventilated and usually doors and windows are open wide. The only time heating might be used is to dry, not heat, the atmosphere during damp or foggy weather, so it is not costly to maintain.

Plants are grown in deep terra-cotta pots and shallow pans according to their requirements. A certain skill and understanding is required, for some of the plants are temperamental, which makes alpine house gardening an absorbing hobby. Some plants are permanent tenants, some are brought in from a cold frame or plunge bed to flower. In February and March I have often seen an alpine house full of flowers, especially when the tiny bulbs like anemones, iris, crocus and fritillarias are blooming. Since these do not respond to forcing in heat

Dwarf dianthuses look charming planted in drifts in the rock garden or beside a path

they are ideal plants for growing in an alpine house.

I am always captivated by tiny annuals. One of the first of these I came to know was *Linaria* Fairy Bouquet — tiny snapdragons, just big enough for a doll's house and easy to grow. A fairy-like little annual sedum is *Sedum coeruleum*, 4 to 6 in. high, with pale green leaves and pretty light blue flowers. The leaves grow red with age and are very attractive.

Almost hugging the ground because it is so small is the violet cress, *Ionopsidium acaule*, which will colonize the cracks between stones if you want it to or carpet spaces in the rock garden. It sows itself generously.

I find some miniatures as amusing as toys; such a one is *Gilia hybrida* which used to be called *Leptosiphon hybridus*. It is well worth growing because the little 6-in.-high plants give a brave assortment of coloured flowers — creamy white, yellow, orange, red, rose and pinks. The tiny Topmix dahlias, perennials in this case, are perhaps the most toy-like of all.

81

Scented Flowers

Few flowers have no scent at all, and the discerning nose may catch a whiff of perfume which is often lost to others. There are even flowers with an unpleasant smell specially designed to attract flies, but these have no place in this chapter!

If you would like to have only scented plants in your garden it is possible to stock it entirely with flowers or foliage that smell sweet – from trees to a camomile lawn. But sometimes what you gain in perfume you may lose in beauty of flower or length of flowering period. The old-fashioned roses, for example, have a perfume often far sweeter than any of the modern flowers but their season is short; after a burst of June glory you are left with a not particularly attractive shrub for the rest of the year. Some, however, like the moss roses and the perpetual-flowering kinds, do give more blooms and some produce lovely, glowing heps in the autumn.

Many of the sweetly scented winter-flowering plants rely on their scent and not on their colour to attract insects. For instance, witch hazel (hamamelis) is no real beauty and the blooms of *Iris unguicularis* are hidden. One of the most sweetly scented of all our winter flowers, a native plant, petasites (winter heliotrope) is best left to grow wild unless you have a very large plot, for you may find you have a weed pest on your hands. Its flowers also are hidden in the great leaves and are no glamour girls!

Some scented and attractive plants for winter are the winter sweet (*Chimonanthus fragrans*), the shrubby honeysuckles (*Lonicera fragrantissima* and *L. standishii*), *Daphne mezereum* (and *D. odora* for the greenhouse), *Mahonia bealei*, *M. napaulensis*, viburnums and edgeworthia, the last for mild districts only.

A few irises will scent the winter air – *Iris unguicularis*, *histrioides*, *reticulata* and *bakeriana* (the last two have the scent of violets), and *vartanii* which smells of almonds. *Crocus vernus*, which begins flowering in February, is very fragrant, one good reason for growing it in pots (see Chapter 16, 'Flowers from Bulbs to Grow Indoors'). October-flowering *C. longiflorus* is sweetly perfumed.

Many of the bulbous flowers described in Chapter 1 have delicious scents. How delightful and unexpected is the perfume of the snowdrops, how powdery and mimosa-like the daffodils and how heady the poet's narcissus and the hyacinths. The Early Single tulips are very sweetly scented, some like Prince of Austria very fragrant indeed. The Double Earlies are rose-like in more ways than one, and the species tulip, *Tulipa persica*, and some of the taller, later varieties all contribute to a scented garden. One bulb merchant offers a collection of scented varieties.

Many of the narcissi, freesias and lilies are gloriously scented bulbous flowers; so are the autumn-flowering *Crocus speciosus* and *longiflorus*, *Ismene festalis*, *Galtonia candicans*, acidanthera, muscari, especially *M. armeniacum* Early Giant. Once very popular and now making a re-appearance is the very fragrant tuberose or *Polianthes tuberosa*. Give it a warm, sunny border.

Thinking of the spring reminds me of violets. When I wrote an article about violets I was touched by the number of readers who wrote wistfully about these flowers they remembered growing wild when they were children and asked if it was possible to grow them in their own gardens. It is, and it is well worth while. They are easily grown from seed and there are several lovely species. Thompson and Morgan of Ipswich have a most comprehensive list of plants, many of them out of the ordinary, which you can grow to scent your garden. However, germination can be slow.

Other perennials, some of which can be raised from seed, are abronia, alyssum, *Aquilegia fragrans* (needs a warm garden), asperula (woodruff), dianthus (pinks and carnations) in variety; monarda (sweet bergamot), *Oenothera odorata* (the perennial evening primrose), peonies, phlox; primulas, especially *Primula auricula*, *elatior*, *polyantha* (polyanthus) and *vulgaris*, the common primrose, as well as *P. chionantha*, *florindae*, *involucrata* and *sikkimensis*; and romneya (the Californian poppy), which will gladden your border and your heart.

So many people have heard of orris root but not all realize that it is dried iris root, from the Florentine iris, *Iris florentina* (syn. *I. germanica alba*). *Iris pallida* is also sweetly scented. These are rhizomatic plants, not bulbs. *Anthericum liliago*, the St Bernard's lily, is a really handsome plant. Lily of the valley can be used to cover the ground and so can the fragrant, fairy-like little hardy cyclamen species. *Polygonatum officinale*, Solomon's seal, is another scented plant for the informal garden.

A fragrant winter flower appearing in January is the dainty *Iris histrioides*

I cannot imagine summer without the unforget-table scent of the mignonette but what a job it is coaxing it to grow! Gardening books tell you that it likes best old mortar rubble, and certainly the only time we had a good prolific crop of it was when we smothered the ground with old mortar from a shed we had pulled down. I now find that the only way I can be sure of it is to grow it in boxes and to prick it out in soil liberally scattered with lime.

As well as mignonette, sweet peas really make my summer. And how wonderful it is to have plants whose flowers *must* be cut, otherwise they just pack up and die! I grow mine naturally either up branching sticks or up one side of the cage over our vegetable garden. I like the modern Galaxy varieties and Unwin's Old Fashioned strain, which really does have the old-world scent.

As I have said elsewhere, I let the little annual alyssum seed where it will because we all love the perfume. But, even so, I always sow some fresh seed in the open ground in late April and again in June. Sometimes, these late-sown plants go on blooming until December.

Other scented annuals are pot marigolds or calendula (but these are pungent rather than sweet), sweet sultans, the night-scented stock and the other larger varieties such as ten-week stock. The night-scented stock is not very spectacular so sow it with something gayer, even something which hasn't a strong scent, and grow it near the house because it is truly heavenly.

Many of the biennials are sweetly scented. Wallflowers are surely the very essence of spring! Others of their family, cheiranthus, will bring other colours at other seasons. *C. kewensis*, the winter-flowering wallflower, is very fragrant. Dame's rocket and Sweet Williams are other perfumed biennials.

Night-scented plants bring real magic to a garden. If you have never grown it before try *Nicotiana sylvestris*, which has candelabras of white, fragrant flowers. The other tobacco flower, *N. affinis*, is also sweet by night. So is *Hesperis matronalis*, the sweet rocket, and another of our wild plants, if you can find a source, *Linnaea borealis*.

The lilies also scent the air on summer evenings. Most of these have a perfume but some are very much stronger than others, the Madonna and regal lilies and *Lilium auratum* in particular. If you have a pool you should grow a scented water lily, *Nymphaea odorata*, and if you have a tropical pool in a green-house you can scent it with lotus flowers.

One of my favourite spots in our own garden is the herb bank which we have gradually built up and covered over the years. It is still growing in height and is becoming prettier and more fragrant every year. Every plant which grows on it is scented — some pungent and herby for cooking, others just for pleasing the senses or for pot-pourri. Among the herbs which have pretty flowers are rosemary, lavender in white, pink and deep purple, Sweet Cicely, tansy, valerian, angelica (smell the root of this), fennel, bergamot, hyssop, santolina, thymes in number but particularly *Thymus citrio-dorus*, the lemon-scented thyme. There are also several mints all of which flower prettily.

We all expect roses to have a perfume but their scents are as individual as the flowers themselves. Where some proclaim their presence with a strong fragrance, others have a faint elusive perfume. If you want roses for their scent alone there are many outstanding ones.

Don't go in for a collection of old-fashioned roses unless you have a large garden because they do take up a lot of room. But make space for a few, especially if you have a spot where they can grow untamed.

A well-stocked herb garden is as much a source of pleasure for its aromatic scent and pretty flowers as for its value in the kitchen

Several nurserymen specialize in old-fashioned and species roses. So it should be possible for you to get almost any one you want so long as it has not gone out of cultivation. *Rosa eglanteria*, the sweet eglantine or sweet briar; *spinosissima*, the pretty little Scotch rose; *centifolia*, the old red Provence or cabbage rose; *gallica*, *moschata*, the musk rose, and many more are those from which you are sure to select some which will win your heart for ever.

The Royal National Rose Society publishes a list of roses including the most fragrant of the modern varieties. My own choice falls on a few. Of the hybrid teas I know and love, I would list Chrysler Imperial, Eden Rose, Etoile de Hollande, Fragrant Cloud, Grace de Monaco, Josephine Bruce, Lady Sylvia, Mme Butterfly, Monique, Silver Lining, Symphonie and Wendy Cussons. Of the floribundas: Dearest, Elizabeth of Glamis, Iceberg, Magenta and Orange Sensation. For walls, Hugh Dickson, Climbing Etoile de Hollande, Climbing Lady Sylvia, Climbing Shot Silk, Royal Gold, Climbing Golden Dawn and Mme Alfred Carrière.

There are so many fragrant shrubs that I cannot possibly list them all but those which come quickly to mind are azaleas, *Azara microphylla*, so strongly vanilla-scented; *Berberis darwinii*, *Buddleia globosa* and *variabilis* with its varieties, *Corylopsis spicata* and *pauciflora*, *Choisya ternata*, *Cassinia fulvida*, the golden bush; *Clethra alnifolia*, the sweet pepper bush; and *Calycanthus floridus* (Allspice) and *occidentalis*.

Lupins, spartium, brooms and gorse are as sweet as the wild clover. *Genista hispanica*, the Spanish broom, is fragrant as are so many of the plants with pea-like flowers. One of the sweetest spots in our garden in early summer is the border with tree lupins, *Lupinus arboreus*, growing in it. The ericas *arborea*, *australis*, and *veitchii* are all fragrant. That lovely shrub, fothergilla, the American witch hazel, ought to be in every garden but it loves a light, acid soil.

Magnolias are almost all perfumed, but you will have to consider the size of your garden. An uncommon member of the magnolia family for a warm, sheltered garden is *Drimys winteri*. Myrtle is a neat shrub for a warm and sheltered spot. The fragrant olive, *Osmanthus fragrans*, will grow in an unheated greenhouse; others need a warm wall.

The mock orange or philadelphus has many varieties. The pyrus or ornamental crabs, apple trees, too, are sweetly perfumed. *Raphiolepis umbellata*, the Japanese hawthorn, is not only fragrant but also a plant for windy gardens.

Sweet-scented wisteria, with its graceful trails of lilac or white flowers in early summer, lends itself to training on a pergola or house wall

Many rhododendrons are beautifully perfumed – including *bullatum*, *formosum*, *fortunei* and *loderi*.

I don't like the scent of elder but I know that many people do, so sambucus must be included. You can get golden-leaved forms which are very handsome. *Skimmia japonica* is a neat evergreen, but the flowers though fragrant are inconspicuous. Good berries follow but you need specimens of both sexes to obtain these.

Some of the species of syringa (lilac) are wonderfully scented and one, *Syringa microphylla superba*, flowers in spring, autumn and, so I have been told, you can be certain of picking blossom on Christmas day. The Persian lilac, *S. persica*, is very fragrant. Many of the modern hybrids are good also – just walk round a nursery at lilac time. Viburnums I have already described in other chapters.

Among the plants that will climb and waft a delicious scent in through your windows are *Akebia quinata*, *Clematis flammula*, *Jasminum officinale*, lonicera (honeysuckle), wisteria and, among the true vines, *Vitis labrusca*, or fox grape.

Flowers for Cutting

If you are lucky enough to have the space, make a cutting patch in which to grow flowers specially for arrangement. This will save you robbing the garden. If you have no room for this there are very many cut-and-come-again plants which you can grow to grace both the garden and the home.

Many plants, herbaceous kinds and annuals in particular, will go on and on producing flowers. If you haven't cut them for arrangement it is important that you remove the flowers from the plants as soon as they have faded so that their energies will not be diverted to making seed and will be used to produce yet more flowers.

Plants like narcissi, tulips and gladioli produce only one or two stems in a season and once these have been cut you will get no more until the following year. Unless you grow great numbers, there will be noticeable gaps when you cut them, and it's worth remembering that they last many weeks longer on the plant than they do in the vase!

Therefore, if you can afford the space and a little extra money, do grow a row or more just for cutting. You can leave the bulbs of narcissi and tulips for at least three years before you lift them — and gladioli corms, too, if you live in the milder part of the country — and then you could use the large bulbs for the border, or for bowls, and replant the smaller sizes for cutting.

Rows of plants are easy to look after. Where these have to be staked, for example, it is much easier to drive in two stakes at each end of a row and support the row with a wire or string running along each side of it. For sweet peas you can use a length of large-mesh wire netting, much more durable than sticks. Very branching plants can be supported by a length of large-mesh wire folded tentwise and placed over the row while the plants are young. They will then grow up through it. This is a good way to grow Bijou sweet peas, border carnations, ornamental grasses and cornflowers.

If you like hardy annuals for arrangements, the following are particularly good: calendulas (pot marigolds); candytuft, clarkia, eschscholzia, godetia, annual gypsophila, linum or flax; larkspurs, annual chrysanthemums and agrostemma (corn cockle). You can get well ahead by sowing them before the second week in September. They will then give you flowers earlier than those sown in the spring and come into bloom before the bedding plants, dahlias and chrysanthemums are ready.

Many plants, including roses, produce flowers in clusters. If you pinch or rub off all the buds except the largest centre or terminal bud, you can usually improve the quality of the remaining flower. Personally, I like to see a nice natural cluster of flowers but, even so, there are occasions when long-stemmed specimen blooms suit your purpose better and to achieve this the flower should be disbudded.

It is no good waiting until the buds are large, for by this time their removal will not alter the quality of the remaining flower. I have a friend who grows a row of Queen Elizabeth roses, a floribunda (or grandiflora as the Americans call this kind of rose), with naturally clustered flowers almost as big as hybrid tea roses. She likes long-stemmed roses for arrangement and disbuds the stems on alternate bushes. In this way she gets really impressive results. Border carnations, chrysanthemums, even dahlias, can be influenced by disbudding.

Another way in which one can influence the quality of the flowers, for instance, chrysanthemums, is by 'stopping'.

Briefly the principle behind stopping is to encourage a plant to make more side branches than it would naturally by stopping it from growing upwards on a single stem. This is done by removing, pinching or cutting out the growing tip. If you have always made a habit of pinching out the shoots of snapdragons or stocks when you plant them in the bedding season, then you have been stopping them.

Chrysanthemum specialists and enthusiasts have special stopping dates to suit each variety. If you want to exhibit your chrysanthemums this is one aspect of their cultivation which you will have to study carefully. Because chrysanthemums are very varied both in season and character, varieties tend to have definite stopping times, ascertained by specialist growers. As a general rule, eight to ten weeks is allowed between stopping and flowering. If you would like to discover more about this on your own the best way is to grow several plants of one variety and treat each one a little differently. But be sure to keep a record of what you do so that you know where you are.

Stopping can also influence the type of flower the plant produces, there being more petals after one stop when the crown buds are allowed to develop than there are when the plant is stopped twice, and the second crown buds produce the bloom.

Carnations grown in greenhouses or pots are also usually stopped and as a general rule they are stopped twice. After the second stopping it takes about six months, all else being well, for flowers to be produced.

The most difficult time for a housewife to find flowers for arrangement is in winter. Here your flowering shrubs will help you but do give the plants a chance to grow before you begin cutting them. Allow three years at least and then make cutting part of the pruning and cut away weak, crossing or too low branches rather than the best.

Many of the flowering shrubs mentioned in my chapter on winter flowers can be cut in bud any time after the shortest day and forced into bloom indoors. If you have a greenhouse, keep a bucket full continuously, even if you cut only a branch or two at a time, so that you always have some to fall back on. Cut the branches on a moist day, not in snowy or frosty weather. Either draw the branches through water, a tank in the green house for example, or spray them with tepid water after you have stood them in deep water.

Always cut them with secateurs, never tear your precious plants, and always split the base of the stem upwards for at least an inch. Don't smash the stem ends with a hammer; this turns the water sour and shortens the life of the flowers. Instead *always* put the stems in warm water at 20°C. (70°F.), baby bath temperature and keep out of draughts, hot or cold.

If you have grown boxes of bulbous flowers (see Chapter 16, 'Flowers from Bulbs to Grow Indoors') consider whether it is possible to pull up the entire flower and arrange it 'on bulb'. If so, you will find that the flowers will last longer. If you cut them, cut them in bud and watch them open indoors. Gather tulips when the colour of the petals is beginning to show, narcissi when the stems begin to bow and make a goose-neck. Irises also should be cut in tight bud; gladioli should have the first 'pip' unfolding. Chincherinchees, lilies, and in fact almost every bulbous flower I can think of, will open in water and live longer this way. Buds do not become damaged like open flowers if you take them on a journey.

Many plants yield not only flowers and buds, but also seed heads, stems and foliage which make interesting flower arrangements. There are also a few plants which produce a good long-lasting crop of flowers which can be continually cut so that you can always have big bowls of bloom *and* bunches to give away. I think that I would put anemones, sweet peas and dahlias at the top of this list.

Anemones respond to a rich, well-drained soil. My own cutting border is raised a little from the path so that it is both well drained and warm. The tubers can be planted at various seasons. In cold, wet districts do not plant before March. Otherwise, plant from January to April for summer flowering and in June for autumn flowers. Plant in September and October for winter flowering. This late crop must be protected by cloches unless you live in a mild district. Always plant the hard little tubers on their edges, 3 in. deep and 4 in. apart.

The glorious poppy anemones include the Giant French or De Caen and the St Brigid strains. St Brigid varieties have the same colours as the De Caen but double or semi-double blooms and curly petals. You can also buy anemones in self colours.

I depend a lot on dahlias for my cottage decoration. If you have no separate bed, these flowers can be grown in mixed borders but make sure that you can get at them to gather them easily. All but the dwarf varieties should be firmly and strongly staked.

Unlike most perennials, a small dahlia plant put in during the first week of June will give masses of flowers at the end of the summer. How many blooms you cut will depend on how well you care for the plants. They need rich or enriched moist soil and some feeding while they are growing. Dahlias are tender and easily killed by frost, so don't be in too much of a hurry! Southern gardeners might be able to get away with planting dahlias in the third week in May but my advice is to wait until the first week in June and then keep them growing by watering them well in the early stages.

Meanwhile order or buy your plants early. Have them ready in a frame and give them plenty of ventilation during the day and cover at night if there is a frost warning. If you have no frame keep the plants outdoors during the day and under cover at night, even if this means bringing them indoors.

Water them well, especially on arrival, and this goes for *all* plants you may buy in or grow. Keep them in their pots. These may be no more than plastic sleeves. Be sure to remove any kind of cover from the roots before planting.

Dahlias can be lifted or left in the ground during the winter according to what part of the country you live in. When frost blackens the stems, cut them down to a few inches above ground level. Carefully lift the whole clump of tubers and store

St Brigid anemones, a beautiful strain for cutting purposes. The St Brigid varieties have double or semi-double blooms

them in boxes of peat in a frost-proof place during winter.

If you have no greenhouse you can divide the tubers and plant them 3 in. deep in garden soil in April. If you do not wish to increase the number of plants you have, merely plant the whole bunch of tubers. Bulb merchants also sell tubers which can be planted in this way instead of young plants raised from cuttings.

If you have a greenhouse with a temperature of 13 °C. (55 °F.) you can start the tubers into early growth. Put them, whole or divided, in pots of soil in March. Keep these growing well and plant outdoors at the end of May or in early June.

To take cuttings you need both a warm greenhouse and a propagating frame stood over the pipes or in the warmest part of the house. Cover the stored tubers with soil in boxes or large pots, in early spring. You do not need to use best potting soil for this: mix half soil, half sand.

Water moderately until the shoots appear. When these are 2 in. long, cut them off almost to the tuber. Re-cut the shoot below the lowest joint and cut off the two lower leaves close to the stem. Insert each cutting half an inch deep in moist sandy soil in the propagator, spaced so that they almost touch. Keep moist at a temperature of 18 to 20 °C.

Finesse Anversoise, a yellow Medium-flowered Cactus dahlia. As well as being invaluable for flower arrangements, dahlias make a colourful contribution to the border

(65 to 70 °F.) but shade from direct sun. They should root after about ten days. As soon as possible give each plant its individual pot. Keep in the greenhouse, moving them farther apart as they become crowded. Harden off in May.

Chrysanthemum cuttings are raised just a little differently. After flowering, cut down the plants, lift the whole root, and pack them tight into a cold frame. Keep free from frost but not warm. At any time after the turn of the year, remove the shoots, trim as for dahlias, and root in sandy soil in pans in a temperature of 10 to 13 °C. (50 to 55 °F.). Young plants can be bought from nurserymen annually for planting out in April. Discard the parent plants. Hardy varieties, such as Koreans, may be divided.

Sweet peas can make a lot of work or be as easy as any other annual. For exhibition they are grown on the cordon system, with a tall, stout bamboo to each vine. Tendrils produced at the ends of the leaves are kept cut off so that no energy is spent. Long stems with many flowers are produced by this method, but you need to give almost daily attention.

Another method is to grow the peas up twiggy sticks in the same way as culinary peas are grown. The disadvantage here is that twiggy sticks are becoming increasingly difficult to find. Wire and other netting is often used instead. I grow my sweet peas up one side of my vegetable cage which is made of wire netting.

Modern varieties of sweet peas such as Galaxy produce long-stemmed flowers with many blooms, quite as good as some exhibition blooms. These are produced naturally and with no special treatment.

Ordinary, but rich or enriched soil and a sunny position are all that is required. The simplest way to grow them is to sow them in rows, in 2-in. deep drills about 3 in. apart. Sow either in March or October, or at both seasons to get a longer crop.

Alternatively, sow three or four seeds in a 3-in. pot in February and transplant in April. If you knock the plants out and carefully disentangle them you will find long roots. Use a dibber when planting; it is much easier than digging a deep hole with a trowel.

Be sure to water the plants well in dry weather or the buds will drop off, and always keep cutting the flowers!

You can plant gladioli in full sun or partial shade and in any type of soil, but they prefer one that is deeply dug and well manured. In heavy soil, place sand beneath the corms.

Flowering times vary according to the kind of gladioli you grow. You can have early-flowering, small-flowered types belonging to various species. Some people beat the seasonal clock and grow these in greenhouses or on the window-sill (see page 118). Outdoors, plant these in autumn and cover the ground with litter or peat against frost, removing the cover in March.

The late-flowering kinds include the dainty-flowered Butterfly race with tall stems but dainty flowers. The Large-flowered kinds are divided into Early, Medium and Late-flowering types. All kinds have colours to suit your home.

Many irises can be found listed among the flowers described in Chapter 1, but here I would like to suggest that you grow the modern Dutch irises for cutting. They bloom in June in lovely colours. Plant them in October in well-drained, gritty soil. You can leave the bulbs in the soil for four years before lifting and dividing.

Suitable flowers for cutting can always be found among the perennial plants in the herbaceous border, many of them lasting well indoors

Dried Flowers for Arrangements

You are almost sure to know the straw daisies or everlastings, which have been popular flowers for winter decoration for centuries, but there are other plants that share this quality of producing blooms with firm, papery petals which do not fade. Most of them are well worth growing and a row or two, even just a few plants in a little garden, will ensure that you have gay flowers right through the winter. I must confess to having dried flower arrangements in my house right through the year. I make a special effort to ensure that the arrangements look as gay and summery as possible, choosing bright containers and pretty flowers, and I also have many green-leaved house plants to complement them. In this way there are always favourite flowers to greet us or our visitors, even if I've been too busy to find fresh flowers. And best of all, they are not affected by heating.

Most of these gay flowers are half-hardy annuals and really quite easy to grow. In some districts you might be able to buy some plants, usually pricked out in boxes during the bedding plant season, but I would advise you to try to grow a few for yourself. Grow them on in boxes or pans, prick out into boxes and then plant outdoors. The seed of many, indeed most, can be bought as mixtures but it is also possible to buy some kinds according to colour so you can make arrangements to suit your home.

In the same way there are many lovely grasses which can be grown to provide graceful shapes to contrast pleasantly with the heavier and circular outlines and forms of the majority of the everlasting flowers and other perpetuelles. There are both annual and perennial species, many of them native plants, which are lovely enough to include in the garden. Farm cereals such as oats, wheat, barley, millet and even rice can be included. It is important that all are cut young. They can also be used first in fresh flower arrangements and then dried, but their colours in this case will not be quite so good although their shape will not be impaired. The best time to gather most for drying is when the flowering portion is just ready to leave, or is freshly emerging from, its sheath. Their colours can then be held.

As well as these real everlastings, there are other flowers which can be dried, known collectively as perpetuelles. Not all of these are as lovely as they are in their fresh, soft state but they really are useful and if you have them to spare, well worth drying.

The drying process itself is important. Gather only on dry days and before frosts. To dry the annual flowers and ornamental grasses you need a shady, cool, airy place. I use one section of our garage where the sun does not penetrate. The flowers should be cut so that any buds or side stems are left on the plant to develop. The foliage, where this is present on the stem, should be stripped and the flowers made into small bunches and hung upside down to dry slowly. Thick, leafy bunches and moist conditions cause mildew.

Most of the flowers retain their stems but some become so brittle that the heads come off. Helichrysums are the worst offenders. For this reason, these flowers are sometimes gathered beheaded and the stemless flowers spread out to dry. Later, false stems are added by piercing flower centres and threading strong grasses or florist's wires down through them.

Alternatively, and this is what I do now for I have found it so much easier, you can cut the flower with just an inch of stem and, while this is still soft, take an 18 gauge, or the finer 20 g., florist's wire and insert it up the short stem until it is embedded in the flower's centre. It should not be noticeable. You will find later that the wires can be easily hidden by other materials in the arrangement. If you wish, it is possible to hide the wire by pushing it down inside hollow grasses. You can also bind it with narrowed (halved), green florist tape. To dry these mounted flowers, stand them in weighted jars, in a dry, airy place until you are ready to arrange them.

Annuals

The following are all annuals you can grow for drying: Statice or limonium. *Limonium sinuatum* in many colours, *bonduellii*, yellow, and *suworowii*, the mauve-pink candlewick statice, are all half hardy. Perennial statice, *latifolium* and *incanum*, both hardy, should be dried in the same way as the others. These two are branching, fine, and not unlike gypsophila in appearance.

Lonas. A little tansy-like, yellow, hardy annual.

Helichrysum bracteatum, or straw daisy. In all colours, heights and sizes; is half hardy. Some of the giant strains are as big as calendula. Cut the daisies as soon as they open, otherwise they will go to seed. Buds may also be gathered.

Helipterum (syn. Acroclinium) and rhodanthe. Half hardy, very dainty daisies in pink, rose and white with yellow or black centres. Their stems are nicely tough, but if reinforcement is necessary use fine wire twined round the stem after being inserted into the base of the flower.

Anaphalis margaritacea and *triplinervis*, the pearly everlasting. Attractive for the silver border. Be sure to cut the flowers young but not immature.

Ammobium alatum, the sand flower. Half hardy.

Gomphrena globosa, Spanish clover. Tender, best grown in a greenhouse unless you live in a very mild district. Cut flowers as soon as they are ready even if this means sacrificing some of the buds. These flowers take a long time to dry.

Catananche, cupid's dart. A perennial and a bit tricky to dry, I find. Cut them while flowers are young and a good blue.

Xeranthemum. Immortelle, white or purple double, daisy-like flowers, half hardy.

Limonium suworowii, the annual mauve-pink candlewick statice, is useful for drying

Ornamental Grasses

Hang them up to dry in the same manner as directed for the flowers. Keep them out of the sun or they will turn to hay. Both annual and perennial grasses can be sown where they are to grow but I find it safer to sow in boxes and plant out the young plants. This way there is no danger of them accidentally being pulled up as weeds.

ANNUALS. *Avena sterilis*, or animated oats; *Hordeum jubatum*, or squirrel-tail grass; *Briza maxima* and *gracilis*, the pearl and quaking grass; *Lagurus ovatus*, or hare's tail grass; *Bromus briziformis*, *Agrostis elegans*, *alba* and *nebulosa*, all fine and feathery. Also half-hardy annuals, to be raised individually in pots in heat and planted out at the end of May, like sweet corn (*Zea mays*) or Job's tears (*Coix lacryma-jobi*).

PERENNIALS. *Anthoxanthum odoratum* (sweet vernal grass); *Phleum pratense* (cat's tail or timothy); *Aira elegans*, grow this species in greenhouse.

Perpetuelles

Among the annuals, perennials and shrubs which produce perpetuelles are the following:

ANNUALS. *Amaranthus caudatus* (love-lies-bleeding) and celosia (cock's comb), nearly related. Both of these should be cut before they are fully mature but not when they are very young.

Salvias. Any of the bedding varieties dry well if this is done quickly.

Dainty *Didiscus caeruleus*, the blue lace flower, coriander, and chervil must be dried quickly.

Zinnias sometimes dry well. The weather seems to have a lot to do with their success. Results are best in hot summers. Support them to keep the shape. Bend a piece of wire netting into a table, and insert flowers through the mesh. Dry quickly, in an airing cupboard for example.

PERENNIALS. *Achillea filipendulina*, yellow yarrow, and *A. ptarmica* or sneezewort, delphiniums – the small spikes are best, belladonnas especially – and *Salvia farinacea* should all be dried quickly, out of the sun. The airing cupboard is a good place. Both echinops (globe thistle) and eryngium (sea holly) should not be cut too young but while the colour is still good. Gypsophila, cut and hang. Solidago

Ornamental grasses are very attractive in dried flower arrangements. This is the hare's tail grass, *Lagurus ovatus*

(golden rod) and tansy, be sure to cut at the right moment: too young they will droop, too old they will go to seed.

Many pompon chrysanthemum varieties will dry, especially the yellow ones. You need to experiment a little.

SHRUBS. Dry all of these quickly as for delphiniums. Buddleia: cut these at their prime. Double heathers dry well. Hydrangeas: wait until the flower heads turn colour and bracts become leathery in texture. Lavender: gather before the flowers become old and drop. Mimosa: just allow to dry (which it is likely to do indoors anyway). Pussy willow can be kept for years if you dry it before the catkins open. Roses, double ramblers and some of the old-fashioned cabbage types will dry.

You can gain a lot of interest and entertainment by trying out a few flowers to see if they will dry. As a general rule, the tougher and more fibrous the texture of the flower the more likely it is to dry. Failing a warm dark cupboard it needs only to be hung in dry circulating air.

Sappy flowers can be best dried in boxes in a mixture of one part of dry, clean sand to two parts of powdered borax or, alternatively, in silica gel crystals, both of which can be bought from a chemist. You need several pounds of silica gel to dry several flowers so that can be initially expensive but you can use it again and again.

By this method one can dry even such sappy flowers as daffodils, dahlias, azaleas, hollyhocks, marigolds, pansies, violets, and roses. Stems may have to be shortened and replaced or lengthened later with false ones.

You need to dry the flowers in air-tight boxes. Either bury them in the sand by pouring it over them as they lie on a bottom layer of it, or, in the case of deep rather than flat flowers, support them on wire netting, fitted into the box. The drying medium must completely smother them. The drying period can only be gauged by experiment, but it is often quicker than one anticipates: some flowers take only three days; left longer they may disintegrate.

Achillea ptarmica The Pearl. This white achillea should be dried quickly, preferably in the airing cupboard

Flowers for Bees, Butterflies and Birds

When I began writing about gardening I had no idea of the many subjects I would need to study and to know about in order to answer the varied interesting questions asked by readers. This chapter is written round three subjects I am often asked about. First, flowers for bees. If you keep bees you will want plenty of the right flowers full of nectar, and pollen near at hand. This is because bees' lives are shortened if they have to fly too far. Fortunately, many of these flowers are very lovely and all are full of character.

Catkin-bearing trees, hazel in particular, plum and other early blossom and early-flowering bulbous flowers will help the foraging workers early in the year. Later all fruit blossom, even the soft fruits like currants, blackberries and strawberries will be visited. (Never spray these bushes if bees live in the neighbourhood.)

Among the many climbers, shrubs and trees they like are: abutilon, acer (maple) species, horse chestnut, amelanchier (snowy mespilus), berberidopsis, berberis (barberry), buddleia, callicarpa, caryopteris, catalpa (Indian bean tree), ceanothus, clematis, *Clethra alnifolia*, coronilla, cotoneasters, daphne, deutzia, diervilla, elsholtzia, escallonia, ericas, fuchsia, gaultheria, hamamelis (witch hazel), hyssop, ilex (holly), lavender, liriodendron (tulip tree), mahonia, malus (ornamental crab apples), passiflora (passion flower), polygonum, potentilla, prunus (which includes ornamental cherries), pyracantha, rhus (sumach), robinia, roses (the single-flowered kinds), rosmarinus (rosemary), senecio (dusty miller), spiraea, symphoricarpos (snowberry), syringa (lilac), thyme, vaccinium (blueberry), viburnum, vitis (vine), and wisteria.

Annual plants include: Alyssum, *Asperula orientalis* (the blue woodruff), borage, centaurea (cornflowers), and sweet sultans, clarkia, cleome, convolvulus, coreopsis, cucumber, echium, eschscholzia, godetia, single gypsophila, iberis (candytuft), lavatera, *Limnanthes douglasii*, linum (flax), malope, single stocks, nemophila (baby blue eyes), nigella, ocimum (basil), phacelia, portulaca, reseda (mignonette), satureja (savory), scabious and tropaeolum (nasturtium).

The bulbs include allium, which means all the onion tribe including chives, which bees (and butterflies also) seem to adore; leeks, shallots and onions in flower as well as the decorative alliums of the border. Alstroemeria, chionodoxa, colchicum, crocus, eranthis (winter aconite), fritillaria, galanthus (snowdrops), hyacinth, leucojum (spring and

Allium moly. Both bees and butterflies are particularly fond of the allium family, which includes onions, leeks and chives as well as these decorative border plants

summer snowflakes), muscari (grape hyacinth), scillas and tulips and others.

Other plants which they like are althaea (hollyhock), *Anchusa azurea*, *Anemone hybrida* (the Japanese windflower), asparagus, aster (the perennial kinds such as Michaelmas daisies), aubrieta, catmint, campanula of all kinds and cheiranthus (including wallflowers), *Chrysanthemum uliginosum* (giant daisy), convallaria (lily of the valley), crambe (seakale), dahlias (the single varieties), doronicum (leopard's bane), *Echinacea purpurea* (the purple cone flower), echinops (globe thistle), epilobium (rose bay), but be careful for this could be a nuisance weed, don't let it seed; eryngium (sea holly), gaillardia, helenium, helianthus, heliotrope, hellebore, hesperis (sweet rocket), inula, lunaria (honesty), lysimachia (Creeping Jenny and yellow loosestrife), lythrum (purple loosestrife), melissa, mints in variety, nepeta, oenothera (evening primrose), pelargonium (pot geranium), phormium (New Zealand flax), polemonium (Jacob's ladder), polygonatum (Solomon's seal), potentilla, rudbeckia,

salvia (sage), saponaria (soapwort), *Sedum telephium*, *S. spectabile*, sempervivum, sidalcea, silene, solidago (golden rod), verbascum, verbena and violets.

Flowers for Butterflies

It is not only because my garden is surrounded by the countryside that butterflies abound, it is also because as the years have passed care has been taken to see that the plants they need are there also. The sight of the first, lonely brimstone in spring is always greeted by us all with joy and we then watch for the first wary tortoiseshells which tell us that longer sunnier days are on the way.

The buddleia is such a favourite plant with butterflies and other nectar-seeking insects that a friend of mine calls the plant the pub-at-the-corner. In late summer mine (I have several varieties of different colours) are coloured with flocks of peacock butterflies which also love to sun themselves on the grass nearby. If you have the patience to stand a little while they will settle on your hand or shoulders and stay, still sunbathing, for many minutes. The buddleia though is not responsible for the presence of butterflies; it merely attracts those which are there already.

Many gardeners associate butterflies with the buddleia bush because they have seen them thick on its flowers. They may think that because of this attraction butterflies breed on buddleias. This is not so. The butterflies could live quite well without this plant. They come to it because the flowers offer nectar. They do not need it for their very existence. But on the other hand should you destroy every stinging nettle in the area you would have few if any butterflies on your buddleia. The stinging nettle is essential to certain lovely species, the gorgeous red admirals, small tortoiseshell, peacock and comma butterflies. The last also likes the nearly related hop and the elm. Their eggs are laid only on this plant and their caterpillars which hatch from the eggs will eat no other leaf. So you can plant all the showy buddleias you like and you would only be offering a snack to a passing butterfly. To do most good you should plan a place for nettles to grow nearby, then you would get the best of both worlds. Other nuisance weeds are similarly essential. Docks and sorrel are host plants to the pretty small copper. The painted lady likes spear thistles. (Finches love the seeds too). Owners of large, isolated gardens could help by providing a weedy area and seeing that it is left uncut until the end of summer, a plot which could be considered a butterfly reserve.

This is just one instance by which you can see that insects are highly selective. They will breed only on certain plants, so if you destroy these you also destroy the insects that are dependent on them. You might not like insects and would not mind if they all disappeared, but then you would have to be prepared to allow most of the birds to die also because they would need the insects for food. They also need seeds and berries of our wild plants. Some animals need all of these also. One thing is absolutely dependent on the other and simply by indulging on overtidyness we are breaking one of the most vital links in the country-side chain.

You might like to know that the dusky Camberwell beauty and the purple emperor butter-flies need willow. The white admiral lays her eggs singly on the fragrant honeysuckle. The holly blue really does lay her eggs on holly and on dogwood and ivy too. Wild or garden thyme is

host plant for the large blue. Other blues, and there are many species of these dainty little gems, like the pretty wild flowers belonging to the pea family. The lovely long-tailed blue likes tree lupins, vetches, broom, gorse and the everlasting pea. Gorse, incidentally, provides a marvellous nesting area for birds. The highly patterned swallowtail needs plants of the cow parsley family and this is a useful tribe for many other insects.

If you find a white butterfly on your mignonette do not mistake it for the cabbage white and destroy it. It will most likely be a Bath white, a migrant which crosses the channel in fluttering clouds in summer.

In spring the earliest species to appear is the pale yellow brimstone. This can be found in my garden, I am happy to say, because the alder buckthorn, its host plant, is there. Appearing a little later are the pretty orange tips which feed on dame's violet, cuckoo flower, Jack-by-the-hedge and honesty, all of which I have growing here. Fritillaries need dog and sweet violets and heartsease.

All of these are pretty plants and deserve to flower in our gardens wherever there is space for them. They have one great thing in their favour.

The handsome sea holly or eryngium is another plant much favoured by bees. This is *Eryngium giganteum*

Bottom: Many attractive annuals and perennials suitable for cutting can be taken from the border without spoiling the garden display. In the foreground of this colourful scene are armeria, clarkia and *Chrysanthemum* Esther Read with eschscholzia, roses, cornflowers and lilies in the background

Opposite left: The summer-flowering gladioli are always popular for cutting. For this purpose they are often better grown in a row in a separate part of the garden

Opposite right: Echinops or globe thistles make a distinctive contribution to a dried flower arrangement. They should be cut for drying while the colour is still good

Opposite bottom: Dahlias are among the most useful flowers for cutting. Tall varieties will need staking, but the dwarf bedding varieties, such as this Coltness hybrid, need no support

As they are natives they are easy to grow so long as they are on the right soil. For instance, foxgloves like an acid soil, and for them to increase naturally you need leafmould and/or peat. On the other hand mignonette must have lime, so sprinkle some on the soil where you want this to flourish. But ordinary soil does very well for the majority of these helpful plants.

If you like butterflies or any other insects it is worth while investing in one of the many good books about these insects. Keep it handy so that you can identify not only the butterfly or moth you see but its caterpillar and also its eggs or egg clusters.

Certainly cabbage butterfly grubs are a nuisance and must be kept down one way or another and so are others which I shall mention, but unless a plant is being eaten to the point of disappearing completely, stay your hand until you have been able to identify the caterpillar. Some, the larvae of moths for example, are likely to be a greater nuisance to the gardener than others.

The surface caterpillars or cutworms which are the larvae of a number of species of moths including the turnip, heart and dart, and yellow underwing moths are particularly annoying. These grubs hide during the day and feast at night on the lower leaves of your plants which they might even sever either just below or above ground level. They also cause plants to wilt and die or to break at the point where they have been nibbled. These larvae are similar to each other, being a dirty grey, maybe tinged with brown, with a row of dark dots along their bodies. The yellow-underwing grubs are larger, more yellow or green yellow and with dark stripes rather than dots along the sides of the body.

These caterpillars appear in late July or thereabouts and as well as your cabbages and root crops of that family, such as turnips, they are likely to attack chrysanthemums and some other members of their family such as annual asters, dahlias, marigolds and zinnias.

Look for them with a torch after dark and keep the ground continually disturbed by hoeing.

Other moths which can do harm are the goat, lackey and vapourer moths. The caterpillars of these are likely to be pests on certain fruit and blossom trees and sometimes on roses. Caterpillars of these either bore into the tree or live in colonies in web-nets on its branches.

Both the larvae of the garden and the ghost swift moths live in the soil. Their grubs are easily identified, being white and shiny with a reddish head. They are fairly active for grubs and tend to move backwards in the hand if you pick them up. They eat many plants including weeds, but they will burrow into certain bulbs, corms and tubers, such as narcissi, gladioli and dahlias, and into the roots of peonies. The moths themselves are quite large, and strangely beautiful. One, as its name implies, is grey and ghost-like. They fly at dusk in midsummer.

There are a few others which cause some damage to fruit trees and bushes but almost all can be kept under control by routine fruit tree spraying.

Fortunately, most of the moths and butterflies are welcome garden visitors rather than pests and will all come to feast at the nectar-producing flowers. I find that they are prettiest in late summer and early autumn when they alight on sedums, Michaelmas daisies, dahlias and globe thistles. They also like many of the plants listed in the section on bees.

Helianthus Soleil d'Or. Bees are attracted to daisy flowers, and the seed heads will provide a welcome meal for birds such as finches

Flowers for Birds

Every November a flock of gloriously coloured bullfinches descend on our beloved winter-flowering prunus and seem to spend hours pecking at the buds. Meanwhile we are torn between the joy of seeing the almost bare branches coloured with these pretty birds and despair because they seem to be ruining the tree. For three winters I watched until I could bear it no longer and crying that the tree would die if they stayed I would rush out and drive them away. But they were not gone for long! Yet our tree, instead of dying, has bloomed for months on end, as I have described elsewhere in this book, longer in fact than any other plant in the garden, including the gorse. (There is a saying that while the gorse is in bloom kissing is in season, so you can guess how long a flowering period this plant is supposed to have!)

At times during the past years we have said to each other, 'Well, it seems that we have to have one or the other, a tree coloured with birds or one coloured with blossom,' but somehow the tree has won. Perhaps all those buds the bullfinches nibbled were full of harmful grubs. Who can tell? I don't want a garden without birds and I learned long ago that you must compromise with them. As I have explained elsewhere, our fruit and vegetables grow under a bird-proof cage. The rest of the plants in the garden they are welcome to. There is no doubt that, their beauty aside, birds are more useful than harmful in gardens. There are those which are exclusively insectivorous, feeding only on caterpillars and insects. Others like the owl are carnivorous, more are herbivorous and some are omnivorous. Sparrows are a nuisance at times of the year when they will peck the yellow crocuses, polyanthus and other flowers for reasons known only to themselves. They do other damage, but they also do their share of clearing the plants of greenfly and other pests. A spray with Morkit will stop them eating plants. It won't stop them having a first taste but it is not harmful, just a deterrent.

I always leave the seed heads on certain plants so that finches of all kinds can find something to eat in winter. Perhaps they will leave better things alone! Michaelmas daisies and daisy seed heads of all kinds, including the decorative thistles, even weeds, will always attract them. I also like to grow a plant or two of teasel for them. Giant sunflowers and some of the smaller kinds also can be gathered and stored away from mice and hung up later, when food is scarce, so that the oily seeds can be pecked out.

Recently goldfinches have increased in numbers and I know that some live in the garden because a pair made a nest in the pear tree right beside the house and we saw them at work. I knew that they came for weed and other seeds, for I have seen them feeding on such plants as dandelions, but I was surprised to see a flock of them one winter's day stripping the old lavender flower heads from the hedge that I had failed to tip after it flowered because I was abroad. Now I don't trim the hedge until spring when all that is left of the previous year's flowers are bare stems.

Almost every red berry will attract blackbirds and others; the alternative here if you want to have berries is to try to find as many yellow-berried plants as possible for these do not appear to have the same attraction. There are, for instance, yellow-fruited holly, viburnum and pyracantha.

Birds in the garden are an endless source of pleasure, and the good they do in disposing of pests more than outweighs the small amount of damage they cause

Top: A lovely spring-flowering shrub which is popular with bees is weigela (diervilla). This is the variety Abel Carrière

Bottom: Golden King, a striking scarlet-berried, variegated-leaved holly

Right: Both the fragrant wisteria and wallflower (cheiranthus) are plants which encourage bees to visit the garden

102

Flowers for Children

My first attempt at growing flowers from seed was so successful that it has remained a vivid memory. My mother drew a circle in newly raked soil and gave me a packet of Virginian stock to sow in it. 'Shake it over carefully like salt,' she advised me. Like the radish to which it is related, this little plant germinates very quickly and even to an impatient child it seemed to flower in next to no time.

Although children love the brightly coloured seed packets, I think it is not wise to let them try to sprinkle the seed from them because this often results in the whole contents landing in one spot. A good way to show them how to sow tiny seeds like the Virginian stock is to let a child scratch his or her initial in the raked, level soil. A really big letter should be drawn. This is best done with a tiny trowel or an old large spoon. Then take out just a little soil so that a shallow drill is made following the lines of the drawn initial.

The soil removed should be put in a sand bucket or a little bowl — there won't be a lot of it! Empty the seed into something that will not be easily tipped over but which is conveniently shaped for little fingers to take the seed out, a pinch at a time. (You can turn a plastic cream carton into a shallower bowl quite easily by pouring boiling water in it and letting it stand for a few minutes.)

Having done this, demonstrate how to sow the seed along the letter drill just a pinch at a time, explaining that you must give each seed room to swell and send its little root down and its shoot up. It also must have room to turn over if it is the wrong way up.

When this is done the soil can be spooned from the bucket to cover the seed and gently patted down to prevent it blowing away. Watering is essential, of course, for the seeds, and, if I know small gardeners, for them too! But see that the watering can has a rose, otherwise the seed might be washed out.

Another little member of the stock family is ionopsidium, a ground cress — very tiny, but so quick growing that it will seed itself more than once in one season. Children also love candytuft (it has a nice name, too), marigolds, nasturtiums (they can safely gather the leaves of these for sandwiches and put flower buds and seeds in salads). The nasturtiums in my own garden are the progeny of the first packet of seed our son planted many years ago. They continue to seed themselves every year. Shirley poppies, cornflowers and godetias are gay favourites. Seedsmen sell mixtures of hardy annuals which I can recommend, and Suttons of Reading sell a children's garden mixture.

If you have more than one child you can organize a sunflower race to see whose plant grows the tallest. Give each a few seeds to sow in March or April. These are large enough to sow individually and the plants are most impressive.

Most children I know love pansies. I think that they see them as little faces. Certainly a little girl I know was seen to offer a bite from a biscuit she had been given to a row of pansies. These flowers do not take long to raise from seed and there is always great excitement when the first bud is ready to bloom.

If the child has his own garden, provide some of the little pansies which seed so freely, such as a variety of *Viola cornuta*. Funny Face is a charming bright mixture producing flowers with little whiskered, cat-like faces.

Give them a violet plant or two so that they have some scented flowers to pick and give away. Sweet peas are useful for the same purpose and nowadays you can find dwarf varieties that need no tall sticks, such as Knee Hi. A good way of supporting these is to fold a piece of wire mesh tentwise and place it over the row or group. The plants will climb up through it and will be well supported.

Some of the dried flowers I have mentioned here might be welcome too. I think I would choose acroclinium. These have a simple, daisy-like, appealing flower, delicately scented. They dry well on their own stems and children would enjoy gathering them, drying them and later even arranging them. A few plants should provide a good bunch of flowers.

A touch of wonder plus the chance to brag is always welcome. Hops are quick-growing climbers and if watered well in the early stages will soon climb a pole. In good soil a single plant of love-lies-bleeding, *Amaranthus caudatus*, will often attain an impressive size and girth and produce great

Iberis umbellata, the pretty candytuft, is an easy plant for a child to grow

Left: Butterflies love sedums and may often be seen resting on the blooms of *Sedum spectabile*, an attractive plant in its own right which flowers in late summer

Top: Pansies, with their little whiskered, cat-like faces, have a special appeal for children and are easy to grow from seed

Bottom: Growing a sunflower is an exciting challenge to a child. The seeds are large enough to sow individually and in a sunny situation the plants can reach an impressive height

Amaranthus caudatus, or love-lies-bleeding, has intriguing tassel-like flowers

A giant pumpkin is fun to grow, especially if the young gardener can be persuaded to water and feed it himself

tassels like velvet chenille. A pinch of Ruby Chard seed will soon develop into plants with enormous magenta-coloured leaves.

Some vegetables are more fun to grow than others. French Breakfast radish, known as Dix-Huits to French gardeners because of the number of days they take to mature sufficiently to be eaten, give a quick return for the minimum of labour. Lettuce, too, can be watched over with pride and finally eaten by the grower himself. If you follow my method and sow the radish and lettuce in the same drill, the radish will germinate first and can be cleared before the lettuce needs the space.

A courgette plant or two might hold the interest longer than a marrow simply because once the fruits form they can be cut frequently. On the other hand, and only where there is room to let the plant have its head, a pumpkin could be dramatic, especially if you can persuade the young gardener to water and feed it frequently.

Some of the new bush-type tomatoes are fun. Give a child a few seedling plants to care for indoors until the time comes to plant them in the garden. Then show how it is best to spray the plants with fresh water from the rose of a can each morning so that the fruits will set. Encourage the child to weigh the fruits he picks and keep a record so that he learns — and marvels at — the total.

Children disdain neat labels and prefer to use the packet to indicate where their seeds are sown. There are two good ways of fixing these so that they don't blow away. One is to split a cane with a knife (you had better do this yourself!), prise open the slit and insert the packet. When the two portions of stick are released the packet is held firm. The other way is to make a slit an inch from the top and bottom in the centre of the packet and thread the stick through the top slit to the back and out at the bottom hole.

Often disappointment is caused by seedlings which don't come up or which disappear. I fear that birds and slugs, snails, and woodlice are to blame more than the seed. A little palisade of sticks and taut black cotton, though not beautiful, is effective against sparrows, and an upturned grapefruit or orange skin will trap slugs.

Bulbs are rewarding but these need patience for

it is a long long time from autumn to spring. A way to give immediate interest is to plant a few autumn crocus (see page 20) when the other spring-flowering types are being planted. These will flower very quickly and by the time they have finished the weather will have changed sufficiently for interest in gardening to have waned.

See also page 112 for bulbs that are easy to grow indoors.

Wigwams of flowers are always popular. A large wigwam will obviously need help from parents unless there are sensible older children in the family, but smaller doll-size ones can be made by the children themselves.

To make them, first draw a circle representing the perimeter of the base on the raked soil. For large wigwams I suggest you cut a circular bed in the lawn leaving the grass uncut on the part of the circle where the entrance is to be. This should be away from the sunniest direction. Canes, poles, pea sticks or twigs (according to the type of wigwam) should be pushed into the soil firmly, a few inches apart – the closer the better for the twiggy ones. All should lean towards the centre at which point they should be lashed together if they are canes, or intermingled if they are twigs. A space should be left for the door. The seed is then sown individually at intervals round the outside near the supports.

For child-size wigwams, use edible gourds; the flowers are large and attractive and the fruit harmless; scarlet runner beans or Blue Coco beans; the first has scarlet flowers, the second violet ones; Galaxy sweet peas or climbing nasturtiums.

For doll-size wigwams grow Bijou sweet peas; sugar peas – these have purple flowers and the pods can be eaten whole; thunbergia (Black-eyed Susans) and convolvulus. You are more likely to get good and quicker results if you wait until April before suggesting seed sowing.

Among favourite perennials that are easy or versatile are Creeping Jenny, periwinkle and stone-crops in variety. Although a hollowed stone can be planted with stonecrops and will soon look pretty, all these plants can be grown aloft rather than on the ground, for instance in a coconut shell.

Make a hole with nails in the shell and use wire to suspend it from a tree. Fill it with a few small stones or sand at the base for drainage and top it with soil. If you like you can paint a face on the nut so that the trailing plant forms the hair. You can add to a child's delight by making a face on each side, a happy one with eyebrows, nose and mouth all U-shaped and a solemn face made simply by painting the same features but all turned down like an upside-down U. Choose a piece of a plant growing in the garden for this purpose and be sure that the plant is well watered.

Black-eyed Susan, *Thunbergia alata*, can be easily trained to form a doll-sized wigwam

Bottom: *Crocus chrysanthus* Advance. Crocuses like this are best raised in a frame and then kept in a cool room until ready to bloom

Centre: A clivia is a beautiful bulbous plant for pot cultivation indoors. It should be regularly watered and fed in summer

Opposite top: The two flowering plants in this charming group, *Begonia hiemalis* and *Saintpaulia* Rhapsodie, blend perfectly with the mixed foliage of *Begonia rex*, *Dracaena* Rededge and *Pteris cretica*

Opposite bottom: Azaleas are popular as presents, but require care to keep them in good condition after flowering

Flowers from Bulbs to Grow Indoors

Many lovely bulb flowers can be grown in pots, bowls and other containers for home decoration. I grow my bulbs in a variety of containers rather than the ordinary bulb bowls. Tulips and hyacinths look much more elegant growing in a stemmed flower vase or an urn. I like to grow the small Roman and Multiflora or 'fairy' hyacinths in baskets which I line with strong polythene to make them waterproof. I use the same kind of lining for many of the copper vessels I like. Daffodils look lovely in a copper preserving pan, and crocuses look sweet in old tureens. An old-fashioned wash basin is a pretty sight filled with hyacinths and a deep china slop-pail suits the long-stemmed, sweet-smelling narcissi Soleil d'Or and Paper White, or Mendel tulips.

Some, like the spring-flowering hyacinths, narcissi, tulips, crocuses and other little bulbs, are only temporary. Once they have been forced to flower early they cannot be grown the same way again and must either be thrown away or planted in the garden where, after two or three years, they will have re-adjusted themselves and will begin flowering again.

Others can be treated as perennials and will spend a lifetime on a window-sill or in the greenhouse. These include nerines, vallota lilies, lachenalias, veltheimia and hippeastrums (often called amaryllis).

Bulbs can be grown indoors in fibre, a soil mixture or a soilless compost. Fibre and the compost are easier for the novice and are suitable for growing entirely indoors, whilst bulbs grown in soil must be kept outdoors in the early stages. Crocuses, irises, some anemones and snowdrops are only brought into the warm to bloom when you can see the colour of the flower petals. These are best grown in frames and moved into an alpine house or cool room indoors. Both fibre and a soilless compost can be used for containers without drainage holes provided you make a drainage layer of crushed charcoal.

Hyacinths, narcissi, tulips and crocuses will all grow in fibre or, alternatively, in soil or a soilless compost. If you want to use them in pretty containers it is possible to grow them on in soil and either pots or deep boxes and when they are in bud gently lift and transplant them into the more decorative vessel.

Keep your bowls filled with only one kind and variety of bulb as otherwise they may not grow evenly. You can plant them as close together as you like so long as they aren't actually touching.

You can buy bulb fibre quite easily or you can mix your own. For this you need six parts by bulk of peat, two parts crushed oyster shell and one part crushed charcoal. You can buy all these at a garden shop. Mix all the ingredients thoroughly and moisten properly before use.

It really is important to moisten bulb fibre evenly. If it is too dry, or if you allow it to become too dry once it is planted, the roots will shrivel. Have it wet enough to cling into a ball when you squeeze it in your hand but not wet enough to drip, and try to keep it like this when the bulbs are growing. It is a good plan to weigh the bowls after planting and when you inspect them during storage to weigh them from time to time to keep the moisture at the original level.

To plant, roughly half fill the bowl with fibre, press it down fairly firmly, and sit the bulbs on this so that when the bowl is filled their noses will be above the fibre level. This way, water is not likely to settle in the centre of the bulb where it might cause rot.

If you are using soil, have a drainage layer of broken flower pot crocks, or, failing these, charcoal nuggets. Once again, let the noses of the large bulbs peep above the soil level. Snowdrops, irises and other tiny bulbs must go deeper in the pot. In soil, daffodils can be set in two layers, one good bulb right at the base of the pot and others grouped over it and round it. This gives you a few extra flowers, for the low central bulb will grow just as fast as the others. Always leave a space between fibre or soil level and the rim of the container for easy watering.

Bulbs will grow quite well in shallow bowls but, if they are the strong-growing kinds, they tend to become a bit of a nuisance if the leaves or flowers flop about. The deeper the bowl the deeper the root hold. Even so, you may have to stake some plants. As a general rule, you need about 3-in.-deep bowls for hyacinths and tulips, deeper than this for all large-flowering narcissi.

Many spring-flowering bulbs can be forced early into flower to provide colourful bowls for home decoration

Successful bulb forcing depends, like pastry, on cool conditions in the early stages. I cannot over-stress that it is very important that filled containers should be stored in a cool, dark place. If you decide to start them off in a cupboard make quite sure that no hot water pipes run through it or near it.

Ideally, and this is the method always recommended by traditional gardeners, the pots and bowls should be kept out of doors during the early stages. They should be plunged in ashes which are well drained, which will deter slugs, or, failing this, in sand or soil. These plunge mediums keep the bulbs naturally cool, dark and nicely moist. But this method just isn't practical for all of us. If you can use it, then make the plunge bed somewhere on the north side of the house. Usually a frame is made to hold the material, but you can use a few deep wooden cases like orange boxes, packed with ashes. Wrap your nice containers in polythene to prevent them weathering or being stained too much.

My own method is an easy one. I either place each bowl or sometimes two or three together according to their size, in a black plastic bag, or I wrap the bowls individually in a piece of black plastic. They are then stood against the wall on the north side of my house. If I have several bowls I make shelves or use orange boxes.

I have learned, to my cost, that you must watch out for mice which will eat crocuses and tulip bulbs, so these are placed in a 'cage' of wire netting. I have an old meat safe which I use effectively. If the bags or wrappings are tightly closed the fibre keeps moist and the plants can breathe through the plastic. The bowls can stay safely wrapped outdoors if you want to bring them in just one or two at a time.

Most people attempt to force their bulbs to flower for Christmas, yet actually there are very few that will flower by that time. Two narcissi, the old-fashioned, very fragrant Paper White and the yellow Soleil d'Or, are naturally early varieties. The Roman hyacinth, technically *Hyacinthus orientalis albulus*, will also flower naturally in November. If you plant the bulbs at intervals you can get a continuation of fragrant, pretty blooms. These three types can all be planted from September to early October. *Crocus vernus* Vanguard will bloom for Christmas as long as it is potted early.

The bulb merchants offer a good range of bulbs specially prepared or treated so that they will flower quickly, often in time for Christmas, but

Narcissus Cragford, a good variety for indoor cultivation

these must be planted early in the season and the directions faithfully followed. They include hippeastrum (as I mentioned earlier, often called amaryllis), hyacinths and some narcissi. I have no doubt that other kinds will be added to this list in time.

Certain narcissi are surprisingly easy. The Tazetta varieties with several flowers on a stem, such as the double Cheerfulness and Geranium, will flower early in the year. Cragford (also mentioned on page 120), and Carlton are grand for indoor culture and there are many others such as the large-trumpeted King Alfred, the double Texas, the single Jonquil, and the pure white Mount Hood. Some of the smaller and miniature forms of narcissi respond to pot culture and grown in this way one has a better chance of admiring the delicacy and sweetness of their little blooms. These are also ideal for an alpine house.

Not really a bulb but treated in much the same way, is convallaria or lily of the valley. The crowns are prepared for forcing and grow very quickly so that you can have them in flower by mid-winter. When you order them be sure to state that you want them for pot culture. Plant the crowns in deep bowls or pots with the tips just above the surface, using a soil mixture or a soilless compost. I like to use six crowns in a '48' (5-in. diameter) pot, allowing about 2 in. between each crown. Water them well and then place them in a warm, dark place (unlike bulbs which need a cool, dark place) – an airing cupboard will do. I turn an empty pot upside down on top of the growing pot (a black plastic bag will also do) and put a cork in the drainage hole to make it quite dark. See that the crowns do not dry out.

After about ten days the shoots should be growing well. When they are about 4 in. high, bring them out and slowly, day by day, move them a little nearer the light. Keep them watered.

If you have a lot of lily of the valley in your garden you might like to pot some to flower in early spring. Either lift a clump which will fit a pot or plant twelve or so large, single crowns in a 6-in. pot. First place a really good layer of drainage material in position and use either John Innes potting soil, a soilless compost, or mix equal parts of good garden soil and leafmould. Place the fitting pots upside down over the planted pots and stand them outdoors in a frame until after the shortest day of the year, then bring them into the warmth and let them grow on naturally in a window or greenhouse. You can bring in one or two pots at a time as they will come to no harm outdoors. Avoid overwatering; wait until you can see that the soil is getting dry.

Tulips are not quite so easy to grow as hyacinths, but they do repay a little care. They like soil best. Allow ten to twelve weeks to elapse after planting and plunging outdoors before you lift or uncover them. Even then, keep them in a dark place with a temperature of about 16°C. (60°F.) to coax the stems to lengthen – this will take ten days to a fortnight. You can then bring them into the living room but not yet into full sun. Introduce them gradually and if your rooms are very sunny it is wise to cover the bulbs with paper – any kind – during the brightest, sunniest period. Exceptions are the Mendels, which can be placed in a light place right away. If you want to use fibre, choose the dwarf early varieties. The doubles remain attractive longer than the single ones.

Only few Darwins will force well and not earlier than February for most of them. The exceptions are William and Rose Copland, both of which are better for greenhouse culture than for room gardening. Grow Early Single and Double and Mendel varieties for early flowers. Some Darwins, such as Demeter, Golden Harvest, Pink Supreme, Prunus and Sweet Lavender and Darwin hybrids such as Apeldoorn, Gudoshnik and Jewel of Spring provide late flowers.

Whereas most bulbs can be brought into gradual warmth almost as soon as you can see the young shoots, crocuses should not be brought indoors until you can see the colour of the flowers. Then they will open really fast. Good bulbs will give you a succession of flowers coming up one after another. I find that you can mix crocus varieties of the large Dutch hybrids (even the yellow) if you use large bowls, but it is unwise to mix other kinds of bulbous flowers because there is too great a variation between flowering times.

Other flowers that you ought not to bring indoors until the last moment are all the early-flowering bulbs, such as snowdrops, muscari, *Iris reticulata* and other early-flowering species, and scillas.

If you would like to have crocuses in the house it is often much better not to try to force them but to lift them from the ground when they are showing colour and plant them in a deep bowl or pot. The exceptions are the *C. chrysanthus* varieties, many of which are yellow and force well.

If you visited an alpine house in early spring you would be captivated by the many lovely little spring bulb flowers growing in thick clusters in pots and pans. There are many of our garden bulbs which are hardy and early flowering but which will, so long as they are not fiercely forced in too-hot atmospheres, beat the clock and give us a taste of spring long before the proper time.

There are others which really can only be grown in the milder areas of these islands. They, too, do not need high temperatures but merely protection from severe weather and a chance to bloom in comfort. If you like unusual flowers I recommend that you try some of these.

If you have a cold greenhouse (in which the temperature is maintained at spring day level, above freezing point, rather than a stove or hothouse, where the temperature is high or even tropical) you can have flowers right through the winter.

If you do not force the plants but allow them to

An interesting bulbous plant for growing in the home is *Hymenocallis calathina*

grow slowly and naturally, they will still flower earlier because of the protection they are given and the bulbs will not be exhausted, and can afterwards be planted in the garden or kept in the same pots.

Bulbous Flowers Suitable for Window-sill Culture the Year Round

All the following will grow in a sunny window in a warm but not hot room or they may also be grown in a cold greenhouse. If it is more convenient, they can be stood outside during summer when the bulbs are allowed to dry, rest and ripen. To ripen the bulbs it is best to lay the pots on their side. All need repotting every four years, and when they are not being repotted they will need topdressing annually. This is done by carefully scraping away the top inch of old soil (do this after the resting period) and replacing it with new. John Innes potting mixture and soilless composts are suitable.

ACHIMENES. The new hybrids of these charming flowers will grow easily in a warm, well-lit room.

Plant from January to May, three rhizomes to a 3½-in. pot or five or six to a 5-in. pot. Cover with about 1 in. of soil. Keep in shade in a temperature of 15 to 21°C. (60 to 70°F.). When the shoots appear above the soil bring the pots into full light, but shade from direct sunlight. Feed when flowers begin to form.

AMARYLLIS (see HIPPEASTRUM).

NERINE. Pot August to November, three bulbs to a 6-in. pot. Water moderately, feed occasionally when flower spikes show. Dry May to September.

VALLOTA (Scarborough lily). Pot newly bought bulbs in autumn or spring. Repot June or July. Plant firmly with bulbs just below the soil surface. Water freely and feed regularly March to June. Dry June to September.

VELTHEIMIA. Plant as for vallota, *Veltheimia viridifolia* August to November, *V. glauca* October to March. Water freely and feed occasionally when in full growth. Allow to dry, keep dry when leaves fade, water moderately when growth begins.

HIPPEASTRUM. Pot January, one bulb to a pot. Let one-third of bulb stay above soil level and allow about an inch of soil all round the bulb, so choose pot according to bulb size. Water freely once growth begins. Give liquid manure when flower spike shows; allow to dry and ripen, and repot each year.

EUCOMIS BICOLOR (pineapple flower). Pot October or March, one bulb to a 5-in. pot. Water very little until March and then moderately to May, freely afterwards. Feed when flower spike shows. Allow to dry after flowering. Repot.

HAEMANTHUS (blood lily). Pot early-flowering species August to November, others March to April; bulbs should be half in, half out of soil. Water only little until growth begins, then moderately. Give liquid manure once or twice a week when flowering. Full sun while growing and resting. Without water after flowers fade.

HYMENOCALLIS CALATHINA. Pot March, water freely until September, moderately until December, keep dry from December to March. Feed weekly May to September.

SPREKELIA FORMOSISSIMA (Jacobean lily). Pot bulbs in February, only two-thirds of their depth. Water freely as soon as growth begins until September. Give liquid feed when flower spike shows. Keep dry after September.

CLIVIA. This needs slightly different treatment because it doesn't die down in the same way. Pot February, water freely and feed in summer. Good light. Topdress annually.

A greenhouse plant which can be brought indoors for temporary decoration, the lovely freesia will fill a room with its distinctive perfume

OXALIS. Pot autumn-flowering kinds in August, winter-flowering kinds in September or October, spring-flowering kinds in March or April; $\frac{1}{2}$ in. deep and $\frac{1}{2}$ in. apart in 5-in. pots. You can grow them on in a window or greenhouse straight away. Water moderately until the leaves begin to grow and then more freely. Give liquid manure when flowers form. Withhold water gradually when flowers fade. Give rest in a cool place until growth begins again. Repot annually.

Bulbous Flowers Suitable for Greenhouse Cultivation which may be Brought Indoors for Temporary Decoration

FREESIA. Pot August to flower in January, October for February, November for March, December for April, in 5-in. pots, 1 in. deep and 2 in. apart. Keep in a cool place; little water until growth begins, then water freely and feed occasionally. Keep warm but not hot. Repot annually.

NERINE (see page 116).

LACHENALIA. Pot August or September, keep in cold frame or cold house, give little water until foliage appears. Bring into warm greenhouse early November, on high shelf near glass. Give weak liquid manure when flower spikes form. Gradually withhold water. Dry June to September.

TRITONIA. Pot 3 in. deep in November. Cover with peat in a cold frame or under staging in cool house until growth begins. Then water moderately until flowers fade. Keep dry to ripen until January. Keep warm but not hot, 5 to 10°C. (40 to 50°F.) in winter.

ZANTEDESCHIA (Arum). Really rhizomes but sold by bulb merchants. Repot annually, August or September single rhizomes in 6-in. pots. Water moderately during winter, freely from March to May. Feed with liquid manure once a week during flowering period. Keep in greenhouse or warm living room in sunny place from October to May, outdoors if possible in summer.

Some bulbous flowers you can grow in pots and either bring into the home, greenhouse or alpine house when they are in flower bud, or, alternatively, they may be left in the frame to flower. All these need plunging or covering and really good drainage. John Innes potting soil, a soilless compost or a mixture of equal parts good loam, leafmould and silver sand may be used. As some are hardy in the very mild parts of the country this indicates that they should be grown as coolly as possible. Give water only when growth has begun, withhold water once the leaves begin to fade. None, except the tecophilaea (see below), can be forced a second time, but they may be planted in the garden. All should be given at least one feed of liquid manure while they are in flower. Most should be planted about an inch apart in small pots, just below the soil.

CROCUS. Blue Celeste, *Crocus chrysanthus* varieties, *C. vernus* Vanguard, large Dutch hybrids in all colours. Pot October to November.

MUSCARI. Many varieties. Pot from August to November.

SCILLA SIBERICA. As above.

TECOPHILAEA (Chilean blue crocus). Pot singly in $3\frac{1}{2}$-in. pots or, alternatively, three to a 5-in. pot, 2 in. deep. Alpine house or frames only. No water until growth is seen.

IRISES. Pot October. Use small pots for the little kinds, e.g. three bulbs of *Iris reticulata* in a 3-in. pot, five of the Spanish and English and *I. tingitana* to a 5-in. pot. Frames and unheated house only for Spanish and English irises. Little heat from January onwards for *I. tingitana*.

SCHIZOSTYLIS (crimson flag, Kaffir lily). Pot November to March. Keep in cold frame, December to April, plunged in sunny border from April to September, place in cold greenhouse September to December. Water freely during summer, moderately at other times, feed occasionally with liquid fertilizer. Repot annually.

LILIES. Lilies may be grown in pots. It is possible to force them into bloom but this really does take a certain skill. Species most suitable for growing in pots are the stem-rooting kinds though some others may be grown. Those recommended for pots and for forcing include species and varieties. They are: the Asiatic hybrids, *Lilium auratum*, *auratum platyphyllum*, *bulbiferum croceum*, *formosanum pricei*, *hansonii*, Honeydew, Jamboree strain, *longiflorum* varieties, *martagon album*, *nepalense*, Potomac hybrids, *pumilum*, *speciosum* varieties, *testaceum* and Verona.

It is best to make a compost of three parts good loam, preferably some which has been stacked for a year (loam is rotted turves), one part flaky beech leafmould (or, alternatively, fibrous peat) and one part clean coarse sand.

You need large pots, a 6-in. pot for a single bulb or a 7-in. or larger for several. It is best not to fill these when planting the stem-rooting kinds but to allow space to topdress the soil so that the stem base is covered as it grows. Plant non-stem-rooting kinds 3 in. deep. Keep the soil just moist until you see the shoots. If the pots are plunged, as recommended, the soil should keep moist enough. Pot from September to March.

Stand the pots on ashes in a cold frame or at the foot of a wall and cover them with ashes or peat, 2 in. deep. When the bulbs are growing they can be brought into a temperature of 7 to 12°C. (45 to 55°F.). Temperatures should go no higher than this unless you really know what you are doing. Keep the bulbs in a light, cool, airy place. The exception to this is *L. auratum* which should be placed immediately after potting in a temperature of 12°C. (55°F.).

The blooms are usually produced about six months after potting. Water the plants moderately until they are in full growth. Then give water freely. After flowering stand pots outdoors and gradually withhold water, except for *L. longiflorum* which should not be kept dry. Repot this species and its varieties annually in September but repot the others in October and November and grow as before.

GLADIOLI. It is possible to grow gladioli in pots,

the late-flowering kinds, three in an 8-in. pot in March and April; the early kinds, five in a 6-in. pot in October to December; all 1 in. deep. Place them in a cold frame until the spikes show and then bring them into a window or greenhouse, temperature 12 to 18°C. (55 to 65°F.). Water moderately at first, freely later. Give liquid manure when spikes show. After flowering withhold water until the foliage dies, then lift, clean and store in trays in a frost-proof place.

ACIDANTHERA MURIELAE. Plant late March to early May, five corms to a 6-in. pot. Keep on window-sill in a warm room or greenhouse. Water freely as the corms grow vigorously, a little at other times. Dry as for gladioli.

BLETIA. A garden orchid of which there are several species; makes a pretty pot plant. Pot in March by just pressing the bulbs in the soil surface. Place outdoors in a shaded place in summer. Bring indoors any time during late summer but shade from mid-day sun. Water moderately August to October. After this, allow plant to dry and rest until March. Repot.

CROCOSMIA. Pot in October, six bulbs in a 5-in. pot. Water when shoots appear. Keep moderately moist. After flowering treat as for gladioli.

CYCLAMEN. Hardy varieties only. Plant 2 or 3 in. apart according to size of corm, and 2 in. deep in wide pans. Water only moderately. Keep in cold frame or cold greenhouse.

Pre-packed Bulbs

I feel that I should mention here the pre-packed Harmony lily and others which are often on sale through mail order and bulb firms.

The bulbs are ready planted in a container, usually one to a pot, and come complete with instructions. As a rule they are available from December to April and of course they make excellent Christmas gifts. I have tried these bulbs and find them easy and delightful to grow. They flower in about eight weeks. The bulb cannot be forced the following year, but like most others it can be planted in the garden where it will gradually recuperate.

The same remarks apply to the bletilla orchid and to the little pleione, both also ready planted. I grew mine on a windowsill with no trouble at all, simply adding water as directed. These pre-packed bulbs are marvellous presents for non-growers, for city people with a love for flowers but no talent with them.

Growing Bulbs without Soil

Most plants must have both soil and water if they are to grow and flower well, but there are some, growing from bulbs, corms and tubers, which, like the camel, carry their own food supply. Just a few of them are so obliging that it is possible to grow them in a saucer or some other suitable container with nothing else at all — no water, no soil!

Quite the prettiest of these is the colchicum (the meadow saffron) about which I have already written in Chapter 1. You will find the bulbs on sale in garden shops in late August and early September.

Do not expect to be able to grow flowers from the same bulb the following year, for it will have had no chance to produce and mature its leaves which follow in the spring when it grows in the garden. However, you can plant the bulb in the garden where it will flower again in time.

The true autumn crocuses, those with grass-like leaves that come with the flowers, will also grow without soil or water, which, to my knowledge, the spring-flowering kinds will not do. Although a saucer may be the handiest container, your flowers will look prettier in some other, deeper container. You can wedge them in place with moss or pebbles.

Another popular no-soil plant is the monarch of the east, whose real name is sauromatum, from the Greek word meaning lizard, a reference to the speckled, lizard-like interior of the flower. It is a member of the arum family. Like the colchicum the sauromatum produces its large inflorescences before the leaves and, again like the colchicum, it will do this while the tubers are merely standing in a bowl. It is a curiosity rather than a beauty!

You can only make this plant flower again another year by potting it in a mixture of half John Innes potting soil and half peat, or, alternatively, in a soilless compost which has a peat base. You should then grow it on like any other house plant. The divided leaves grow on nicely speckled stems.

Other bulbs are so simple that all you need to bring them into bloom is water. You are all familiar with the hyacinth growing in a glass. I once judged a competition where all the members of a Women's Institute had to grow one bulb in a 1 lb. preserving jar. The results were varied and most were extreme-

Acidanthera murielae is another desirable bulb for raising in the greenhouse or on the window-sill of a warm room

ly good. Almost any kind of glass vessel will do for this purpose as long as the bulb will sit firmly and not topple over when the plant is heavy with flower. The old-fashioned, specially designed hyacinth glass or modern copies are ideal as they have a flared portion at the top in which a bulb will sit.

The water should not come right up to the base of the bulb but should be just below it. A few nuggets of charcoal will keep the water sweet. All bulb roots should be encouraged to grow well and quickly. One of the reasons one sometimes sees funny little squat hyacinth flower spikes with the leaves towering round and above them, instead of the lovely flower spikes which are desired, is because they have been forced into bloom before the plants have grown enough roots.

The charm about growing hyacinths in glasses is that you can watch the roots sweeping round the glass as they elongate, but, even so, you should hide the bulb away in the dark until those roots really get moving. Except when they are well in bud never grow bulbs in the warm. Choose a cool place to begin with. Remember that bulbs in the garden spend months in the cold, dark soil before they begin to grow, so try to reproduce similar conditions in your home.

If for some reason you just have to grow the bulbs in glasses on a window-sill, then try to choose the coolest spot to begin with, even outside the window if this is safe, and cover the entire lot, bulb and glass, with either a black polythene bag or, alternatively, a cone like an old-fashioned dunce's cap, made of dark paper. Let this remain on until the roots have grown down into the water by which time the little shoot will just be showing in the nose of the bulb. Don't be impatient! Go on growing the bulb on your coolest or least sunny window. Turn it by a half turn every day so that it grows evenly and do not bring it into the warmest place until you see the colour of its flowers.

Otherwise, store the glasses in a cool, dark cupboard into which no daylight penetrates, or put them, covered with brown paper or black polythene, in a cool shed or in a box placed on the north side of the house.

Hyacinths are sold in various sizes as well as in different varieties. You will also see prepared bulbs on sale; these have been treated or given an artificial winter so that they flower quickly. I suggest that you don't buy the specially prepared bulbs for glass culture. You will find that the cheaper, smaller size will give good results and will stand firmer in small containers, although the top-size bulbs will, naturally, give larger flowers.

I have grown many bulbs in water (you can sometimes find tiny crocus glasses), including many varieties and types of narcissi, but although these flower well they often present problems because their leaves flop about and they have to be tied.

Taller plants like these need a firm anchorage and, fortunately, it is possible to supply this very easily by growing the bulbs in bowls filled with pebbles or any small cleaned stones. Any bulbs which grow in plain water will also grow in pebbles, which, of course, must be kept moist. For some years now I have grown fine narcissi (the variety Carlton in this case) in bowls filled with pieces of broken flower pot and household china. But pebbles look nicer! Some narcissi, the early-flowering Cragford for example, force better in pebbles than they do in fibre or soil.

Use a few charcoal nuggets strewn at the bottom of the container. Pack the pebbles to about half the depth of the bowl, stand the bulbs on this and wedge them in position with pebbles so that they have their noses well above the stones and also well above the rim of the bowl.

I saw an unusual use for hyacinth glasses once when I was in Holland. The showy anthurium plant (not a bulbous plant, incidentally), was growing this way. The strong throngy roots had been washed of soil and they were visible through the glass. Grown this way the anthurium needs feeding with a soluble plant food.

Many leafy plants (those with leafy stems as opposed to the bulbs) can be increased by taking cuttings which one can root easily in water. Perhaps the best known of these is the pretty Busy Lizzie, really *Impatiens sultanii*. But what many non-gardeners may not realize is that it is possible to let the plant go on growing in plain water. Here again you need pebbles or very coarse sand for anchorage. Once the plants have rooted and begun growing you should feed them with a soluble plant food for the water will not contain any. This mode of culture is a very simple and domestic form of growing plants known as hydroponics.

It's fun mixing little water-rooted cuttings. Others you can try are nasturtiums, the flowering tips of small-flowered begonias, any flowering succulent stems such as echeveria which will become plants. Use an unusual and attractive container for them — an old deep meat dish, a lidless teapot, or a tureen, and don't forget the charcoal!

Flowering House Plants

My home is full of house plants. The longest lived are grown mainly for the beauty and shape of their foliage. Few of these flower, or if they do, the flower is of little consequence. The peperomia, for example, sends up a crop of green rat tails which are as unlike one's conception of a flower as you could imagine! Generally speaking the flowering plants which we grow indoors are temporary tenants because many of them are annuals. Any perennials are often treated as annuals or grown in such a way that it is difficult to keep them developing once they have expended their energies in flowering.

We get many flowering plants at Christmas or Easter and, because they are gifts, it is only natural that we should wish to keep them for as long as possible, even for another year. Often this is possible but only under certain conditions – clean air, warm rooms, good light without sunlight, rain water and understanding care are the main requirements.

Often, as with azaleas and cyclamen, we are advised that the way to try to keep a plant is to let it spend the summer out of doors, but not everyone has the space to do so. For some years now I have been keeping these plants indoors the year round, taking special care of them. In summer I spray the leaves and keep them clean, or rest the plant. I find that there is really little difference between plants treated in this way and those which have been stood out of doors, so don't worry if you have neither a garden where you can plunge azaleas and solanums, nor a frame for cyclamen.

The main thing to realize is that in most cases a plant in flower in a pot is flowering out of season and in order to do this it has to be grown artificially. Just as any bulbs which have been forced will not produce again until they have had time to readjust themselves, a process which may take two or three years, so often a forced pot plant cannot quickly – and sometimes will never – get back into a natural cycle. Therefore, it is often best to treat it like a bunch of flowers which has given you good value and to throw it away when it's past its best. On the other hand if you have time, and/or a greenhouse, you might enjoy trying to keep the plant.

Sometimes it is possible to take a cutting from the plant and to grow this on while you discard the parent. Pelargoniums, for example, make neater, stronger plants begun anew like this than if you try to keep them.

If you like indoor gardening there are several plants which can be grown from cuttings. Some, like the impatiens or Busy Lizzie for example, root easily in water. Once they have made roots you can plant them in soil. Cuttings that root easily in water, as well as some others, will root equally well in moist sand or in a mixture of peat and sand. They need to be potted on into good soil mixtures once the roots are made so that the plant foods are available to them. Alternatively, keep them in the sand and peat mixture and feed them regularly.

Some other plants can be divided. In this case you need to knock the entire root from the pot and gently tease it apart so that it falls into defined plants. Saintpaulias (African violets) often need dividing after they have been growing in the same pot for some time. You can tell when a plant needs attention because the crown, the portion where roots and top join, is so obviously in several parts and not a single crown any longer.

If you particularly like a pot plant which you have always found difficult to keep when it has been given you as a mature plant, try raising some from seed. You are likely to be more successful. I find that cyclamen and African violets do best when they haven't been moved from one environment to another and you can raise them on a window-sill. Impatiens, primulas, begonias (the small-flowered fibrous-rooted kinds), exacum, a lovely fragrant little flower, and heliotrope, are other examples. Don't be impatient if the seeds do not germinate quickly, and if only a few should show do not throw away the contents of the seed pan, more may follow.

I sow all of mine in bought seed compost or seed soil mixture in earthenware seed pans. The soil is made moist but not sodden, the seed being sprinkled thinly on the top and only just covered, unless there are directions to the contrary. The pan is then put inside a transparent plastic bag, which is inflated and then closed tightly at the mouth. I usually slip the label inside the elastic band I use to fasten the bag. This bag acts as a little propagating frame. I stand it in a warm place, usually on a window-sill over a radiator, but you can use the airing cupboard so long as you move the pans out into the light directly the seeds have germinated. The bag is kept closed until the seedlings have three leaves and then they are pricked out to roomier quarters, but you can let them stay on a little longer so long as they are not crowded.

If you haven't managed to get the soil just correctly moist you may find that there will be a great deal of condensation inside the bag. A little is desirable but too much may cause damping off.

In this case, remove the bag and merely turn it inside out and replace over the pan. Do this more than once, if necessary.

Many annuals can be grown in the greenhouse or indoors, some of them through the winter months when they are most welcome. These have to be short-day plants, originating from countries where the sun sets early. In most good seed catalogues you will find a selection of plants suitable for greenhouse culture. Sowing times vary according to the plants but almost any time is seed time.

A great deal depends on what sort of home you can offer them. My cottage window-sills are very wide because the walls are thick. They face south and west which means that the light is good. Although, I must hasten to point out, glaring sunshine does not suit all plants and if your windows are very sunny you would be wise to hang a fine net curtain between the glass and the plants.

Any annual which can be grown in a cold greenhouse, as opposed to a hot or stove house, can be grown on a sunny or well-lit window-sill in a warm room. As I write I have cyclamen, calceolarias, mixed impatiens, schizanthus, fibrous-rooted begonias, and glorious coleus, all of which have been raised from seed also sown and germinated in pots on the window-sills. At other times I have had heliotrope, mignonette, alyssum, streptocarpus, morning glories, acroclinium and rhodanthe (these little everlastings make charming pot plants), cinerarias (these are very susceptible to greenfly), solanums, as well as many foliage plants, all raised from seed and grown in this way.

One thing that I cannot cope with are the numerous pots which are necessary if you prick out every seedling to its own pot, which is standard practice. There is just not enough room for this, and over the years I have found a way which is not only successful but results in very attractive decorations. I use bowls, dishes, flower vases and other vessels, none of which have drainage holes. In each I place a really good layer, half an inch to an inch deep, of crushed charcoal as drainage. A large bag-full is very cheap and it can be used time and time again. I used always to use John Innes potting soil mixture and I also use a soilless compost because I find that there are no watering problems. If I have to be away and someone else looks after the house, I can say, 'Please water the plants when you see the surface is dry' (something I dare not say when they are growing in soil) for it is almost impossible to overwater this compost. It is also very light in weight and clean to handle.

I have been amazed at how well really vigorous plants will grow in not very deep containers. Sometimes I have as many as a dozen plants in together. They are never allowed to starve, for after pricking out when they have grown sufficiently to be touching each other, we begin feeding them with a soluble plant food. This is given in a weak solution but regularly. Incidentally, it is always most important to follow the directions on feeding very carefully and to give less rather than more.

Of course, if you prefer it, you can grow these annuals in ordinary flower pots. Large plants such as the tall schizanthus are usually given a pot to themselves after they have been pricked out into smaller pots and gradually moved on as their roots have outgrown the size. Never make a big jump in pot sizes but just move the plant up to the next size. Smaller plants, such as the acroclinium or mignonette, are pricked out to five plants round the rim of a 5-in. pot. It is as well to push in some branching twigs at this point so that the plants will grow through and be supported. Alternatively, use thin sticks and raffia or fillis.

Several annuals do well raised from seed in pots on a sunny window-sill, including the coleus shown here with its highly coloured leaves

Some seeds are so tiny that they are almost invisible, but others can be easily handled either with fingers or tweezers. If you wish, you can save time by sowing these individually in their permanent containers. I often do this and I use potting compost for all but the top inch, when I use seed-sowing compost. I allow about an inch between the surface and the rim of the container for watering at some later stage, and I tie a piece of transparent plastic over the top of the container, as though I was covering a jam jar. I know that we are usually advised to cover germinating seeds with dark paper until germination takes place, but I never do.

But what about the ready-made pot plants you receive? Perhaps the following notes will help you care for them.

Plants need humidity and this is lacking in most homes. A good and convenient way to supply it is to plunge the pot plant inside another container which is large enough to take a layer of peat or some similar moisture-retaining material below, around and (in the case of plastic pots) a little over the actual soil surface. If this plunge material is kept constantly moist but never sodden the air round the plant will also be moist as the water evaporates.

You may still have to water vigorous plunged plants (azaleas for example) in the usual way, pouring the water in so that it fills the space between soil level and the rim of the plant pot. But usually the roots will take what they need from the moist material surrounding them for quite long periods.

It is also as well, especially if you have several plants, to invest in a little atomizer which will spray a fine mist over the leaves. Many of the plants enjoy this. Keep the spray off the flowers unless you are sure that these will not become discoloured. Try to use rain water for watering and syringing plants. If you keep a jug standing about in the home it will be at room temperature, which is better than using cold water.

Now let me tell you in detail about some favourite pot plants.

AECHMEA. One of the easiest. Keep the vase made by the leaves filled with water; feed through the soil fortnightly in summer. Pot offsets separately when parent plant dies.

ANTHURIUM (palette plant). Give it a warm room, good light, sponge leaves; can be divided. Water freely in summer, moderately in winter.

AZALEA. Never allow root ball to dry out, best plunged, use rain water. Warm place, good light, out of sun. Feed fortnightly when in bud, repot after flowering to size larger in peat.

BEGONIA, large-flowered, raised from seed. Good light out of sun. Water freely in summer and feed while in flower. Gradually withhold water when flowers finish. Rest in winter, re-start early spring.

BEGONIA, fibrous-rooted. As above, except that they do not die down.

BEGONIA, tuberous-rooted, large-flowered. Start tubers in February or March in shallow boxes filled with peat or leafmould in temperature of 18 to 21°C. (65 to 70°F.). When rooted pot individually in small size, later transfer to larger pots. John Innes potting soil or a soilless compost. Water moderately, freely later and feed. Shade from sun. Rest tubers after flowering.

BELOPERONE (shrimp plant). Plunge but do not make soil too moist, maximum light; feed moderately while in flower.

BOUGAINVILLEA. Not easy, humidity essential; give plenty of light, warmth, and spray air around plant.

CALCEOLARIA hybrids. Temporary. Give plenty

Cape ericas require constant moisture and dislike draughts. Though attractive in the home, they tend to be short-lived

of light and keep warm. Water, and feed liberally.

CHRYSANTHEMUM. It really all depends on what kind, but most pot plants are year-round types grown under very artificial conditions. Plant in garden and hope for best after it has finished in house.

CINERARIA. Watch for aphid under leaves. Give plenty of water. Once the plant wilts it never seems to regain its turgid stems. Feed regularly while in flower.

COLUMNEA. Give as much light as possible; mine grows at right angles to a French window. Water freely in summer. Feed lightly when in flower.

CYCLAMEN. Will die if any fumes, gas, oil, or smoke, pollute the atmosphere. Needs cool, never hot, conditions and plenty of light. Water from the base or by plunge method, never over the corm. When leaves fade, rest the corm keeping soil almost dry; topdress and start into growth again at end of summer. Feed when buds appear.

ERICA (heath). Usually killed by drought. Keep soil constantly moist. Give cool, airy conditions but no draughts. Use rain water for watering and daily spraying; unlikely to last for long.

EUPHORBIA BOJERI (crown of thorns). Treat as a cactus (which it is not). Give plenty of sunshine, keep warm. Water once a week and feed regularly in summer, water once monthly in winter.

EUPHORBIA PULCHERRIMA (poinsettia). Now available all the year round. Roots must be kept constantly moist. Dislikes too warm or fume-polluted air. Good light but no sun. Resents sudden changes of temperature. Cut stems right back after flowering to second bud from base.

FUCHSIA. Not really happy in living rooms. They need as natural conditions as possible. Spray lightly daily. If they sicken stand them outdoors or plant in garden. Allow to rest in winter by keeping almost dry. Cut right back to base in February and begin watering.

GARDENIA. Keep warm but syringe foliage lightly often. Spraying is more important than watering. Soil must not get too wet. Avoid moving the plant around. I grow mine in a fireplace 6 ft. away from a good window.

GLOXINIA. Keep plants cool in summer, good light but no sun. Good ventilation but no draughts. Never allow soil to dry out. Water from below. Feed while in bud and flower. Keep water off leaves and flowers. Allow tuber to rest for winter. Repot in February.

HOYA CARNOSA (wax flower). Warmth is essential. Water freely in summer. Plunge in moist peat.

HYDRANGEA MACROPHYLLA HORTENSIA. A particularly thirsty plant. Dislikes dry air. Give plenty of light, feed when buds show. Can be planted outdoors or kept in pot. Cut back stems in spring to two good buds.

HYPOCYRTA (goldfish plant). A good tough plant. Keep roots fairly moist. Feed in summer.

IMPATIENS SULTANII (Busy Lizzie). Give plenty of water but let the soil dry out fairly well before filling up again. Give less water and more warmth in winter. Feed regularly when in bloom. Pinch out for tidy shape.

KALANCHOE. An easy plant. Give plenty of water in summer, less in winter. Feed before it blooms.

PELARGONIUM (pot geranium). Hates any kind of unclean air! Give light and sun. Give little water in winter but plenty in summer. Feed regularly in summer but don't grow in too big a pot or it will make foliage at the expense of flowers.

PRIMULA. Plenty of water, regular light feeding when in flower; warmth and light, no sunlight or dry heat.

SAINTPAULIA (African violet). Hates fumes. Plenty of water in summer, moderate in winter, warm, moist conditions, good light but not direct sunlight. Keep water off leaves.

SCHLUMBERGERA BUCKLEYI (Christmas cactus). Give plenty of light but not sunlight and not long artificial light in evenings. Water freely in summer (you can stand it outdoors then), moderately in winter except when it is in flower, when it should have plenty. A light feed when it is about to flower. Spray occasionally. Grows well plunged.

SOLANUM (winter cherry). Water carefully and regularly, spray daily. Keep cool, good light, feed weekly.

SPARMANNIA AFRICANA. Easy, plenty of water in summer, takes almost any situation.

SPATHIPHYLLUM. Keep always in shade. Give plenty of water and food, even in winter.

STEPHANOTIS. Keep warm; mine grows in a south window. Water generously in summer, keep on dry side in winter. Spray leaves.

Index